University of Essex   Library

Date Due Back

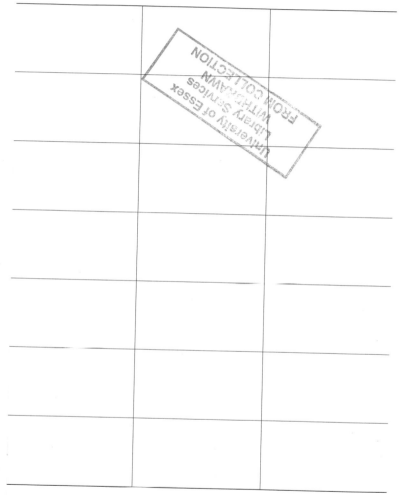

Books may be renewed online (or telephone 01206 873187)
Unless they have been recalled.

Form No. L.43 April 2004

D0309146

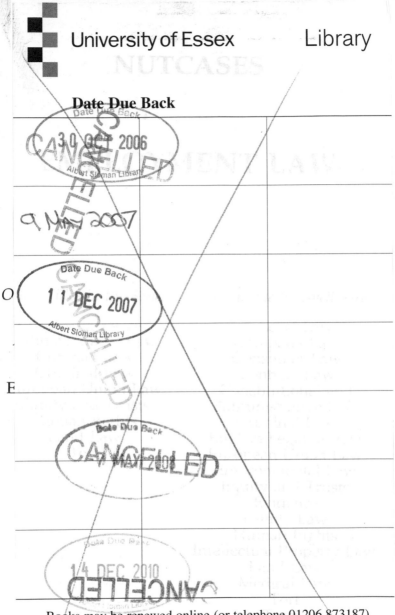

AUSTRALIA
Law Book Co.
Sydney

CANADA and USA
Carswell
Toronto

HONG KONG
Sweet & Maxwell Asia

NEW ZEALAND
Brookers
Wellington

SINGAPORE and MALAYSIA
Sweet & Maxwell Asia
Singapore and Kuala Lumpur

NUTCASES

EMPLOYMENT LAW

SECOND EDITION

by

ANDREW C. BELL
Lecturer in Law
Nottingham Trent University

London · Sweet & Maxwell · 2004

First Edition 2001
Second Edition 2004

Published by Sweet & Maxwell Limited of
100 Avenue Road, Swiss Cottage, London, NW3 3PF
www.sweetandmaxwell.co.uk

Phototypeset by
LBJ Typesetting Ltd of Kingsclere
Printed in Great Britain by CPD Wales, Ebbw Vale

No natural forests were destroyed to make this product:
only farmed timber was used and replanted

ISBN 0 421 87100 8

**A CIP Catalogue record for this book
is available from the British Library**

©
Sweet & Maxwell
2004

CONTENTS

LIST OF ABBREVIATIONS

CAC	Central Arbitration Committee
CCT	Compulsory Competitive Tender
CO	Certification Officer
DDA	Disability Discrimination Act
EAT	Employment Appeals Tribunal
ECJ	European Court of Justice
EDT	Effective Date of Termination
EPA	Equal Pay Act
ERA	Employment Rights Act
HSE	Health and Safety Executive
RRA	Race Relations Act
SDA	Sex Discrimination Act
SOSR	Some Other Substantial Reason
TULR(C)A	Trade Union and Labour Relations (Consolidation) Act 1992
TUPE	Transfer of Undertakings (Protection of Employment) Regulations 1982

TABLE OF CASES

TABLE OF STATUTES

1. EMPLOYEE STATUS

Defining the Relationship

Key Principle: The question of employee status is only out-lined by statute (s.230 of the Employment Rights Act 1996), to decide the issue the courts have developed a succession of tests: the Control test (*Yewens v Noakes 1880*), the Integration test (*Cassidy v Ministry of Health* 1951), the Multiple or Economic Reality test (*Ready Mixed Concrete* 1968) and the Business test (*Market Investigations* 1969); the more recent approach, however, has been to consider each case on a holistic basis (*Hall v Lorimer* 1994, *Lane v Shire Roofing* 1995).

Yewens v Noakes 1880
The case concerned the employment status of a senior clerk for the purposes of the Workmen's Compensation Act. The Act drew distinctions between manual workers and other "profes-sional" workers, rather than the modern day "employees" and "independent contractors".

Held: (CA) The clerk was a "professional" rather than a "servant". In his judgment Bramwell L.J. stated "a servant is a person who is subject to the command of his master as to the manner in which he shall do his work". (1880) 6 Q.B.D. 530.

Commentary
Most of the factual aspects of the case are no longer relevant due mainly to the numerous changes in the law since the case was decided. However, the issue of control has remained a central feature in decisions of employment status; Cooke J. stating in *Market Investigations* (1969) "... control will no doubt always have to be considered, although it can no longer be regarded as the sole determining factor." Likewise, more recently, the House of Lords in *Carmichael* (1999) stated that a sufficiency of control is an essential element of a contract of employment.

Cassidy v Ministry of Health 1951
The case concerned the employment status of a hospital doctor. Since a doctor has specialist skills which an employer could not be expected to directly control, the application of the test from *Yewens v Noakes* would not be appropriate.

Held: (CA) In holding that the doctor was an employee, Somerville L.J. suggested that an employee was a worker whose work was integral to the business, whereas the work of an independent contractor was only accessory to the business. [1951] 2 K.B. 343.

Commentary
The test was used by Lord Denning in the case of *Stevenson Jordan & Harrison v MacDonald & Evans* [1952] 1 T.L.R. 101, but is very difficult to apply sensibly today; is the work of a canteen assistant integral to the business of a paint manufacturer? On the other hand, many functions considered integral to a business may be subcontracted out to specialist companies or individuals.

Ready Mixed Concrete (South East) Ltd v Minister of Pensions and National Insurance 1968
The driver of a concrete mixer lorry, previously employed on a contract of service, was re-engaged as a self-employed independent contractor under a very different set of terms and conditions. He was to purchase his vehicle, which was painted in the company's colours, on hire-purchase from the company, he would be responsible for the running and maintenance of it, he would only use the vehicle for delivering the company's products, he would wear company uniform, would be subject to general control by the company, be paid according to the work he did without deduction of income tax or national insurance, and if he was unable to work, he should hire a suitable replacement driver to ensure that the vehicle was available to the company.

The Minister claimed that the company were liable for national insurance payments, maintaining that the driver was an employee.

Held: (QBD) The court considered all the factors, and held that, on balance, the terms of the contract were more consistent with a contract for services than a contract of service. Thus the driver was an independent contractor. MacKenna J. stated that a contract of employment would exist if three conditions were satisfied: firstly, that the worker agrees for a wage or some other consideration to provide his own work or skill; secondly, that the worker agrees that when carrying out the work he will be subject to some extent to the other party's control; and thirdly, that the other provisions of the contract are consistent with it being a contract of service. [1968] 2 Q.B. 497.

Commentary
On the facts of this case, application of any of the earlier tests could have resulted in the decision going either way. Two issues appear to have swayed the court: firstly, that the driver, and not the company, carried the risk of profit or loss; and secondly, that the driver could sensibly be viewed as running his own haulage business. This test has, in effect, been reinforced by the House of Lords decision in *Carmichael v National Power plc* (1999), so that it may now be read as:

(a) Is there a sufficiency of control over the worker?

(b) Is there a contractual relationship giving rise to a mutuality of obligation?

(c) Are the other terms of the contract consistent with it being a contract of employment?

Market Investigations Ltd v Minister of Social Security 1969
The company, involved in market research, employed both its own permanent staff and also a number of other interviewers on a part time or temporary basis, as required by the workload. The minister claimed that all the workers were employees, thus the company were liable for national insurance contributions on their behalf. The company maintained that the temporary or casual workers were self-employed.

Held: (QDB) In holding that the workers were employees, the court asked whether the worker was in business on their own account. If "yes" then the worker was self-employed, if "no" the worker was an employee. In deciding the question the following factors are relevant: the issue of control, although not by itself conclusive, should always be considered; does the worker provide his own equipment; does he hire his own helpers; what degree of financial risk does the worker run; what degree of responsibility for investment and management does the worker have; and how far does the worker profit from the sound management of his work. [1969] 2 Q.B. 173.

Commentary
In many respects this case is merely an extension of the *Ready Mixed Concrete* principle. It does, however, highlight the fundamental question of whether the worker is in business on his/her own account. In the later case of *Lee v Chung*, the Privy Council, although doubting that any test would be suitable for all situations,

did suggest that the approach adopted in *Market Investigations* was to be preferred.

Hall (Inspector of Taxes) v Lorimer 1994

Mr Lorimer was a skilled audio-visual technician working in the television industry. Due to the nature of his work, many of his assignments were short term—some lasting no more than a day. Whilst on an assignment he did not generally supply his own equipment and he worked under the overall control of the client company/employer. He wished to prove his self-employed status so that he could offset expenses against his income. The Inland Revenue disputed his claim, arguing that he was an employee of each of the companies he worked for.

Held: (CA) In holding that Lorimer was self-employed, the Court of Appeal agreed that deciding a worker's employment status was not a matter of merely running through a series of mechanical tests, but rather of looking at all of the facts and making "an informed, considered, qualitative appreciation of the whole". [1994] I.R.L.R. 171.

Commentary

The court was apparently influenced by the large number of separate engagements Lorimer had undertaken—some 580 in 800 days—and the short duration of many of them. This would appear to be a common sense decision, despite the fact that Lorimer did not have any investment in equipment, made no financial contribution and took no risk of profit and loss as detailed in *Market Investigations*.

Lane v Shire Roofing Co Ltd 1995

Mr Lane was a self-employed roofer. He was retained by a roofing company and paid on a price per job basis. Whilst working from a ladder tiling a porch roof, he slipped and fell, sustaining serious head injuries. He maintained that the company should have provided him with scaffolding from which to work, and thus they were negligent. The company argued that Lane was an independent contractor, and consequently they were not liable.

Held: (CA) The court held that Lane was in fact an employee of the company. The court apparently felt that, although there was evidence to the contrary, the deciding factor was the question: "Whose business was it?" With regard to the overall project being undertaken, the answer must be that it was the company's, not Lane's. [1995] I.R.L.R. 493.

Commentary
The case concerned issues of health and safety; case law suggests that had the central issue been one of unfair dismissal or redundancy, the court may well have viewed things rather differently.

Key Principle: **The contract of employment is essentially a personal contract between the employer and the employee.**

Express and Echo Publications v Tanton 1999
Mr Tanton was employed by the company until he was made redundant. Some time later, he was re-engaged as a driver on a self-employed basis. A term in his contract stated that should he not be available to perform any of the required duties he should arrange at his own expense for a replacement worker. Although Mr T did not sign the agreement as he did not find this clause acceptable, he did continue to work for the company, and on occasion provided a substitute worker when he himself was unable to work. He later complained to a tribunal that he had not been provided with a statement of his employment terms and particulars as required by s.1 of the Employment Rights Act 1996, claiming that he was an employee.

Held: (CA) As there were factors indicating both employee status and self-employed status, the tribunal had performed a "balancing act" and found that the factors indicating employee status outweighed those suggesting self-employed; thus Mr T was an employee, a finding that was upheld by the EAT. The Court of Appeal, however, found that the inclusion of a substitution clause in the contract was fatal to the argument that the contract was a contract of service, thus Mr T was not an employee. As Peter Gibson L.J. stated, "... where, as here, a person who works for another is not required to perform his services personally, then as a matter of law the relationship ... is not that of employee and employer." [1999] I.R.L.R. 367.

Commentary
This judgment reinforces the personal nature of the employment contract, an issue that was influential in the *Ready Mixed Concrete*

case. It has been suggested that the decision is open to abuse by employers inserting a substitution clause into what would otherwise be a contract of employment, and thus escaping liability for the worker. Although such a course of action is theoretically possible, it is perhaps unlikely that most companies would themselves find such a clause acceptable. (See also *McFarlane v Glasgow City Council* [2001] I.R.L.R. 7.)

Key Principle: **The intention of the parties is merely a factor to be taken into account, it is not in itself decisive.**

Ferguson v John Dawson & Partners Ltd 1976

Ferguson worked on the company's building site as a labourer. It was agreed between the parties that he would work on a self-employed basis: "... there were no cards, we were purely working as a lump labour force." Whilst working, Ferguson fell from a flat roof, which was not protected by guardrails, and suffered serious injuries. He claimed damages for breach of statutory duty from the company; they responded that he was self-employed and thus the relevant part of the legislation did not apply, as it concerned employees only.

Held: (CA) In a majority judgment, the court held that Ferguson was an employee. The company had the right to exercise control over Ferguson, they provided him with necessary tools, and he was paid on an hourly basis, which the court felt was correctly described as a "wage". The majority held that any declaration by the parties as to Ferguson's status should be disregarded if the other contractual terms indicated employee status. [1976] I.R.L.R. 346.

Commentary

It is apparent that Ferguson's status as self-employed was little more than an attempt by the parties, instigated by the company, to reduce their financial liabilities—using independent contractors will normally be more financially advantageous than employing staff directly. Furthermore, since the issue concerned a health and safety issue it is perhaps not surprising that the court found as they did.

Massey v Crown Life Insurance Co 1978

Between 1971 and 1973 Massey worked as an employee of Crown Life as manager of one of their insurance offices. In 1973 he was advised by his accountant that it would be financially beneficial to him to change his status to self-employed. He proposed this course of action to his employers who agreed. A new contract was drawn up which was very similar to the original one, except that Massey was to be paid a gross figure and be responsible for payment of his own taxes. The Inland Revenue were agreeable to this change. In 1975 Massey was dismissed, and sought to claim compensation for unfair dismissal—which he could only do if he was an employee.

Held: (CA) Distinguishing the case of *Ferguson v John Dawson* on its facts, Lord Denning held that Massey was in fact an independent contractor. Lord Denning confirmed that if the true relationship of the parties was one of employer and employee, they may not change that relationship by merely applying a label to it; however, in the present case the parties relationship was perhaps ambiguous, and in such a case the parties may remove that ambiguity by their agreement. Famously, Lord Denning stated "Having made his (Massey's) bed as being self-employed, he must lie on it." [1978] 2 All E.R. 576.

Commentary
Although at first glance this judgment appears to be in conflict with *Ferguson*, it is very possible to reconcile the two. Ferguson was a labourer who had little alternative but to accept the job on the terms offered, whereas Massey was a manager, already employed by the company, who took professional advice before changing his status so as to benefit himself financially. It would appear to have been unfair to allow Massey the financial benefits of self-employed status whilst working, and then to have allowed him the benefits of employee status once the employment was terminated. It should perhaps also be remembered that *Ferguson* concerns a health and safety issue, whereas *Massey* concerns purely financial matters.

Key Principle: **Employment status will normally be an issue of fact for the tribunal to decide.**

Lee v Chung 1990
A stonemason was injured whilst working on a construction site in Hong Kong. The company claimed he was self-employed,

and thus they were not liable for him. It was agreed that the company provided the tools for him, told him where to work, but then allowed him to work unsupervised and paid him for the work completed. If there was no work for him, he was permitted to work for other companies.

The first question for the court, however, was whether it had jurisdiction to hear the appeal, which it would normally only have if the issue was a question of law, rather than of fact.

Held: (PC) The Privy Council approved the test from *Market Investigations* and held that the workman was an employee.

On the question of whether employment status was an issue of fact or of law, Lord Griffiths stated, "Whether or not a person is employed under a contract of service is often said ... to be a mixed question of fact and law. Exceptionally, if the relationship is dependant solely upon the true construction of a written document it is regarded as a question of law ... But where ... the relationship has to be determined by an investigation and evaluation of the factual circumstances in which the work is performed, it must now be taken to be firmly established that the question ... is to be regarded by an appellate court as a question of fact to be determined by the trial court." [1990] I.R.L.R. 236.

Commentary
This view by the Privy Council supports the Court of Appeal decision in *O'Kelly v Trusthouse Forte* (1984) that employment status is generally a question of fact for the tribunal, and as such it is not open to an appellate court to interfere. The two exceptions to this are when the status turns on the interpretation of a document, as in *Davies v Presbyterian Church of Wales* (1986), or if the decision reached by the tribunal was "a view of the facts which could not reasonably be entertained" (*Edwards v Bairstow* (1956)).

Atypical Workers

Key Principle: **The status of part-time or casual workers in some situations is still uncertain.**

O'Kelly v Trusthouse Forte plc 1984
The company operated the Grosvenor House banqueting hall, and relied heavily on the use of casual workers to staff large functions. There were two lists of casual staff—approximately 100 regular casuals, of whom Mr O'Kelly was one, and some 250 other casuals who were used less frequently. Mr O'Kelly was dismissed along with others for trade union activities. He claimed unfair dismissal, the company argued that such a claim was not available to him since he was a self-employed independent contractor.

Held: (CA) The court in effect drew up three lists: a list of those factors which indicated employee status, a list of those factors which were not inconsistent with employee status, and a list of those factors which were inconsistent with employee status. In holding that O'Kelly was not an employee but an independent contractor, the court placed greatest weight on the lack of mutuality of obligation in the relationship—is the company obliged to offer work to the worker, and is the worker obliged to accept work offered. [1983] 3 All E.R. 456.

Commentary
Although this case has attracted considerable academic criticism, it is still good law and regularly cited as authority to find that casual workers are not employees. Apart from the fact that the test of mutuality of obligation is extremely difficult for any casual worker to satisfy, in *O'Kelly*, it may be argued, the test was satisfied, in that if Mr O'Kelly wished to remain on the preferred list of casuals he was obliged to accept the work that was offered to him. It appears that the courts (especially following the House of Lords judgment in *Carmichael*) apply the test of "mutuality of obligation" as a contractual test, and as such by the very nature of the relationship, it is virtually impossible for casual workers to satisfy it.

Nethermere (St Neots) Ltd v Taverna and Gardiner 1984
Both Mrs Taverna and Mrs Gardiner had been directly employed as garment workers by the company. By 1979, however, both were working as "homeworkers", working at home, using the company's sewing machines and paid on a piecework basis. Neither had any fixed hours and both were able to decide the amount of work they would undertake, subject only to it being worthwhile for the company driver to call to pick up and deliver. Following a dispute in 1981

concerning holiday pay, both Mrs Taverna and Mrs Gardiner sought to complain of unfair dismissal. The company resisted their complaint arguing that neither were employees.

Held: (CA) By a majority the court found that both home-workers were employees, Stephenson L.J. stating: "I cannot see why well founded expectations of continuing homework should not be hardened or refined into enforceable contracts by regular giving and taking of work over periods of a year or more and why outworkers should not thereby become employees ..." [1984] I.R.L.R. 240.

Commentary
Although this case was heard shortly after *O'Kelly*, the test of mutuality of obligation was apparently not strictly applied. In his dissenting judgment, Kerr L.J. stated that he could find no authority that even a lengthy course of dealing could convert itself into a contractual relationship. The decision, however, is to be welcomed by extending employment rights to a category of workers who otherwise would be left totally unprotected by legislation.

Recently, *Raymond Franks v (1) Reuters Ltd (2) First Resort Employment Ltd* [2003] I.R.L.R. 423, the Court of Appeal has again adopted the approach of considering whether a course of dealings may give rise to a contractual relationship.

Carmichael v National Power plc 1999
Mrs Carmichael worked as a guide for National Power, on a "casual as required" basis, showing groups of visitors around Blythe power stations. She worked some hours most weeks for a number of years, wore a company uniform, on occasion was provided with a company vehicle and had many of the benefits of full-time employees. Mrs Carmichael complained to the tribunal that she had not been issued with a statement of employment particulars as required to be given to all employees under s.1 of the Employment Rights Act 1996. The company responded that Mrs Carmichael and other casual workers were not employees for periods during which they were not actually on site working for the company; in other words no "umbrella" or "global" contract of employment existed. The Court of Appeal had earlier held that in this case the issue of employment status was a question of law as the relationship could be decided by interpretation of the various documents, and further

that application of a slightly mollified test of mutuality of obligation—is the company obliged to provide a *reasonable* amount of the work available, and is the worker obliged to accept a *reasonable* amount of the work offered—indicated that she was an employee.

Held: (HL) Their Lordships allowed the appeal by National Power and held that Mrs Carmichael was not an employee. They stated that no obligation to either provide or accept work existed—the only obligation was merely a moral obligation of loyalty and such a moral obligation was insufficient to prove the existence of a contract of employment. Furthermore, the House of Lords held, the Court of Appeal were wrong to consider the documentary evidence in isolation when considering the issue of judicability, they should instead also have considered the factual circumstances and the intention of the parties. [1999] 4 All E.R. 897.

Commentary
This decision reinforces the approach taken in *O'Kelly* and further strengthens the importance of the test of mutuality of obligation. It should, however, be noted that the employee status of Mrs Carmichael, when actually performing her duties as a guide for National Power was not questioned. The issue in this case was whether an overall or "global" contract existed which was effective during periods when Mrs Carmichael either chose not to be available for work or when no work was available to her. Consequently, it is very possible that Mrs Carmichael may have worked for National Power as an employee under a series of short contracts of service; what the House of Lords have made clear is that without firm mutuality of obligation, no ongoing contract of employment may exist for casual workers.

———————

Key Principle: **Agency workers may or may not be the employees of the recruitment agency.**

McMeechan v Secretary of State for Employment 1997
McMeechan had been on the books of an employment agency for several months, during which time he had completed several assignments for them. The agency became insolvent and McMeechan sought to recover from the Redundancy Fund set

up under s.122 of the Employment Protection (Consolidation) Act 1978 unpaid wages due to him from his last assignment. Such recovery could only be made if McMeechan was an employee of the agency. Previous case law (*Wickens v Champion Employment* (1984) and *Pertemps v Nixon* (1993)) indicated that agency workers were not employees.

Held: (CA) The court held that an agency worker may have the status of employee of the employment agency in respect of each particular assignment undertaken, even though the worker may not have an ongoing or "global" contract of employment. For each assignment the test to be applied is that of mutuality of obligation, and in respect of each assignment it is likely that this test may be satisfied. [1997] I.R.L.R. 353.

Commentary
This appears a straightforward decision, in line with the major authorities. Many of the earlier employment agency cases had been brought to try to prove the existence of a "global" contract, rather than a contract of service for each individual assignment. It appears that at times the courts had confused the two issues and felt themselves bound in all agency workers cases by previous "global" contracts decisions.

Montgomery v (1) O & K Orenstein & Kopple Ltd and (2) Johnson Underwood Ltd 2001
Mrs Montgomery worked for some two years, through a recruitment agency Johnson Underwood, as a receptionist at the premises of O & K. When she was dismissed by JU at the request of O & K she sought to pursue a claim, which she could only do if she was an employee. Mrs Montgomery claimed that she was an employee of JU, but if that was wrong, then she was an employee of O & K. Both JU and O & K disputed the claims, each arguing that Mrs M was not their employee. The EAT held that Mrs Montgomery was an employee of Johnson Underwood, the agency. Johnson Underwood appealed.

Held: (CA) The Court of Appeal held that the approach to adopt was that of the test from *Ready Mixed Concrete v Minister of Pensions* (1968), adapted by the House of Lords judgment in *Carmichael v National Power plc* (1999). Consequently it was necessary to first show a sufficiency of control and a contractual mutuality of obligation between the parties before considering other factors in the relationship. Since there was insufficient evidence that the EAT had considered these issues, the Court of Appeal held that the EAT had made an error of law, and the appeal by Johnson Underwood should succeed. [2001] I.R.L.R. 269.

Commentary
This case is worth reading in its entirety, as it details the various, sometimes conflicting, authorities in this area of law, and demonstrates the problems faced by tribunals in reaching decisions when dealing with agency staff.

Although both a sufficiency of control and contractual mutuality of obligation may exist, in an employment agency situation it is unlikely that they will exist between the same parties. Day to day control is normally exercised over the worker by the client company, whereas it is the agency that will have a contract (and therefore may have mutuality of obligation) with the worker. It is, however, important to remember that whether there is "a sufficiency of control" and whether mutuality of obligation exists, will be a question of fact for the tribunal (see *Dacas v (1) Brook Street Bureau & (2) Wandsworth LBC* [2003] I.R.L.R. 190). Furthermore, in the case of *Raymond Franks v (1) Reuters Ltd (2) First Resort Employment Ltd* [2003] E.W.C.A. Civ. 417, the Court of Appeal implied a contractual relationship between the agency worker and the client company, based at least partly on the long duration of the assignment, thus allowing a tribunal to find that the worker was an employee of the client company rather than the agency.

---

2. CONTRACT OF EMPLOYMENT

Section 1 Statement

Key Principle: **The Section 1 Statement is not a contract of employment.**

System Floors (UK) Ltd v Daniel 1982
Mr Daniel was initially employed as an agency worker with System Floors. He then transferred to System Floors as a direct

employee, at which time he was issued with a statutory statement of terms and conditions (a section 1 statement). He signed
the statement to acknowledge receipt. He was later dismissed
and sought to rely on the statement to prove his starting date—
which he could only do if the statement amounted to a contract.

Held: (CA) The statement, although providing strong *prima
facie* evidence of the contents of the contract of employment, is
not in itself a contract. [1981] I.R.L.R. 475.

Commentary

In most cases the statement of terms and conditions and the
contract of employment will be contained in the same written
document. However, if the contract of employment is not issued as
a written document, or if it does not contain all the information
required by s.1 of the Employment Rights Act 1996, a separate
written document must be issued—in most cases this document
will not amount to a contract.

Gascol Conversions Ltd v Mercer 1974

Mr Mercer was employed by Gascol on a 54 hour week, made
up of 40 hours basic and 14 hours overtime. Following the
introduction of the Industrial Relations Act 1971, which obliged
employers to issue all employees with a statement of terms and
conditions, Mr Mercer was asked to sign and return a document
confirming that his basic hours were 40 per week, which he did.
When he was later made redundant he argued that his redundancy pay should have been calculated on the basis of a 54 hour
week.

Held: (CA) Since the document he signed was headed "Contract of Employment", and since he had signed to confirm
receipt of the contract, he was bound by it. Thus his redundancy
pay was calculated on his basic working week of 40 hours.
[1974] I.C.R. 420.

Commentary

This is a quite straightforward decision, and along with *System
Floors* demonstrates the difference between a section 1 statement
and a contract of employment. It also demonstrates the importance to the parties of the actual wording used in the document.

Terms and Conditions of the Contract

Key Principle: **The products of collective bargaining may be incorporated into the individual contract of employment.**

Robertson v British Gas 1983
Mr Robertson's letter of appointment stated that "Incentive bonus scheme conditions will apply...". He later received a statement which confirmed that incentive bonuses were to be calculated in accordance with the rules of the scheme currently in force. Some time later, British Gas terminated the collective agreement between themselves and the trade union. Withdrawal from the collective agreement by British Gas meant the loss of considerable bonus payments to Mr Robertson and he successfully sued British Gas in the county court for the loss of earnings. British Gas then appealed to the Court of Appeal.

Held: (CA) As the terms of the collective agreements had been incorporated into the individual contracts of employment, they could only be removed by the agreement of the parties, not by a unilateral declaration by the employer. [1983] I.C.R. 351.

Commentary
Although the products of collective bargaining between an employer and a trade union are not legally binding between those parties, those products will be binding between the employer and individual employees if there is an express statement in the contract of employment to that effect. If there is no express term in the contract it may be possible to argue that they are incorporated through implication, in effect through custom and practice.

Burton Group v Smith 1977
Mr Smith had applied for voluntary redundancy under a scheme negotiated between his employer and his trade union. Although a date for redundancy had been agreed between Burton and the union, Mr Smith died before notice had been served on him. In order to be eligible for the redundancy payment his estate needed to show that the union had been acting as his agent and thus notice had in effect been given to Mr Smith before his death.

Held: (EAT) Although a union may act as agent for its individual members, to do so it would require a specific agency agreement. An agency agreement does not stem from the mere

fact that the individual is a member of the union. [1997] I.R.L.R.
351.

Commentary
In most cases it is very unlikely that either the individual or the
trade union would wish to have a specific agency agreement in
place. It is of course possible, by using such an agreement, for an
individual to appoint any third party to act as agent.

Key Principle: **It is possible for terms to be implied into a
contract of employment through custom and practice.**

Sagar v H Ridehalgh & Son Ltd 1931
Sagar was a weaver whose weekly wage was calculated in
accordance with agreed principles based on the amount and
type of cloth woven. On the occasion in question the company
deducted an amount in respect of three yards of cloth contain-
ing a fault which rendered it unmerchantable—although such
deductions were not included in the agreed principles.

Held: (CA) As it was the established practice in this mill—and
indeed in many of the mills in the area—to make such deductions for substandard work brought about by lack of care on the
part of the employee, such a term was implied in the contracts
of employment. [1931] ChD 310.

Commentary
The court made two further comments: firstly, that the sum should
not exceed the actual cost of the defective cloth, and secondly, that
the deduction did not amount to a deduction from ascertained
wages; rather, a deduction in the calculation of wages.

Key Principle: **Generally, there is no duty on the part of the
employer to provide work.**

Collier v Sunday Referee Publishing Co 1940
Collier worked as a sub-editor on the Sunday Referee newspaper. Whilst there was still over a year to run on his contract,
the newspaper was sold to new owners who did not require

Collier's services. His original employers retained him, continuing to pay his wages on condition that he appeared at the office on a regular basis, even though there was no work for him. In an action for breach of contract, Collier contended that the company had a contractual obligation to provide him with work.

Held: (KBD) The court held that only in exceptional cases was there a duty to provide work: where the worker is paid on a commission basis, or where the contract contains a term, perhaps implied, that the bargain includes publicity. Famously, Asquith J. stated: "Provided I pay my cook her wages regularly she cannot complain if I choose to take any or all of my meals out." [1940] 2 KB 647.

Commentary
The exceptions would include those working on a commission basis who would receive no wages if they were not permitted to work; those who would regard publicity as part of the remuneration package, actors, singers, "personalities", etc; and presumably those who need to continue to perform their job in order to retain certain skills (surgeons perhaps) and probably those who need to keep up to date in fast moving markets or high technology industries—although see also the section on "restraint of trade".

Devonald v Rosser & Sons 1906
The plaintiff worked in the production department of the defendant's factory. He was paid on a "piece-work" basis, receiving no fixed salary but paid according to the amount of work he produced. When the factory closed down, the employer gave Devonald the required contractual notice of dismissal. However, they argued, as he did not have an agreed salary, they were not required to pay him for the notice period.

Held: (CA) In the case of piece-workers, the court held, the employer has an implied duty to provide the employee with work. However, that duty is not absolute, it may not apply in cases of machine breakdown, lack of power or materials, etc. but it would apply, whilst the contract existed, if the employer's argument was simply that he could no longer make a profit on the work. [1906] 2 K.B. 728.

Commentary
A further exception to the general rule in *Sunday Referee Publishing*.

Langston v Amalgamated Union of Engineering Workers 1974

Langston was employed by a UK motor manufacturer and had refused to join the trade union. Following protests from the union, the employer, rather than risk confrontation with the union, continued to pay Langston's wages but required him not to attend for work. As a preliminary issue under what is now repealed legislation, the court had to decide whether the union had induced the employer to commit a breach of contract. The question therefore was whether paying wages but refusing to allow the employee to work may amount to a breach of the contract of employment.

Held: (CA) "... these days an employer, when employing a skilled man, is bound to provide him with work. ... the man should be given the opportunity of doing his work when it is available and he is ready and willing to do it."—*per* Lord Denning M.R. [1974] I.C.R. 180.

Commentary

Three points may be noted:

(1) The case was heard in a time of general industrial conflict, following the Industrial Relations Act 1971, and may be thought to reflect the views of Lord Denning, rather than a concensus statement of the law at that time.

(2) In the earlier case of *Hill v CA Parsons & Co Ltd* [1972] Ch 305, referred to in *Langston*, Lord Denning had stated; "If the company did not want him to come to work, the court would not order the company to give him work."

(3) When *Langston* came before the NIRC for a full hearing, rather than adopt Lord Denning's reasoning, the court held that Langston was a piece-worker, and thus the exception to the general rule, detailed in *Devonald v Rosser*, applied.

William Hill Organisation v Tucker 1998

Mr Tucker had been employed by William Hill for over 10 years. In 1996 he had agreed to a contractual term which required him to give up to six months' notice should he decide to terminate his employment. In 1998 Mr Tucker was offered and accepted a position with another organization within the same industry, and gave one months' notice of termination. William Hill required him to abide by the contract term and give six months' notice, but stated that although he would continue to receive salary for the notice period, he was not required to attend for work, and should consider the six month notice period as "garden leave", during which time, of course, he would not be permitted to take up alternative employment. William Hill applied for an injunction to enforce the contract but this was refused by the High Court on the grounds that since Mr Tucker's contract did not contain a specific "garden leave" clause, his employer had a duty to provide him with work during his notice period. Their failure to do so amounted to a breach of contract, and consequently Mr Tucker could accept the breach as terminating the contract. William Hill appealed.

Held: (CA) Although there was no accepted right to work, there was in some circumstances a duty on the part of an employer to provide work in a situation where the employee needed to exercise their skills. This, the court held, was such a case; the appeal would therefore be dismissed. [1998] I.R.L.R. 313.

Commentary
See also the issue of "Restraint of Trade".

Key Principle: **An employer has a duty to pay wages. With very few exceptions, failure to pay the full amount due is actionable by the employee as an unlawful deduction.**

Delaney v Staples (t/a De Montfort Recruitment) 1992
Delaney was dismissed and given a cheque for money in lieu of notice. The company then stopped payment on the cheque claiming that Delaney had taken confidential information from the company, and they were therefore entitled to dismiss without notice. Delaney then complained to a tribunal that the failure to honour the cheque amounted to an unlawful deduction of wages.

Held: (HL) Money in lieu of notice is not normally regarded as "wages" since it is not remuneration for work done during the employment; rather, it is damages payable for the breach of contract which occurs when the dismissal takes place without the required notice period. [1992] I.C.R. 483.

Commentary
Unless there is a contractual condition allowing for termination of the contract by payment of monies in lieu of notice (see *EMI v Coldicott* [1999] I.R.L.R. 630), payment in lieu of notice will not be regarded as wages. However, payment of outstanding bonus or holiday pay is considered to be wages.

The other issue arising from *Delaney* is that a total failure to pay wages is also a "deduction" of wages, and thus of course actionable.

Miles v Wakefield Metropolitan District Council 1987
Mr Miles worked as registrar of births, marriages and deaths, working a 37 hour week, including conducting civil weddings on a Saturday morning. As part of an industrial action organised by his trade union, Mr Miles refused to conduct weddings on Saturday morning, although he continued to work 37 hours per week, including Saturday mornings, and carried out all his other duties.

His employer made it clear by letter that if he refused to conduct weddings on Saturday mornings he would not be paid for those Saturday mornings, even if he attended at his office and carried out other work.

At the end of the dispute Mr Miles applied to a tribunal to reclaim the monies withheld for the Saturday mornings, claiming unlawful deduction of wages.

Held: (HL) Mr Miles' claim failed. His refusal to carry out his agreed duties amounted to a breach of contract. Furthermore, his offer of partial performance of his contractual duties was refused by his employer in their letter to him; thus the employer was entitled to refuse to pay for those hours. [1978] I.R.L.R. 193.

Commentary
This view of partial contractual performance was taken a stage further in the following case.

Wiluszynski v Tower Hamlets LBC 1989
As part of an industrial action, Mr Wiluszynski, a housing officer, refused to carry out a very small part of his contractual duties, although he attended work and conscientiously carried out all his other duties. His employers, however, had advised

him that if he was not prepared to carry out all of his duties he should not attend work, but if he did, any work he undertook would be regarded as voluntary. At the end of the month long dispute Mr Wiluszynski applied to a tribunal to recover his wages for the entire period, all of which had been withheld by his employer.

Held: (CA) The employer had made it clear that part performance of the contract was not acceptable, even though they had permitted Mr Wiluszynski to continue to perform his other duties. Therefore they were not obliged to pay for any of the work that he performed during the period of part performance. [1989] I.C.R. 493.

Commentary
This may be seen as a harsh decision, especially since the employer had taken no steps to prevent Mr Wiluszynski from carrying out his other duties. However, since the employer had made their position clear, and since the failure of the employee to carry out the full contractual duties clearly amounted to a breach of contract, the decision is fully supportable.

Key Principle: **There is no general right to payment of wages when the employee is absent through sickness.**

Mears v Safecar Security Ltd 1982
When Mr Mears received his section 1 statement there was no mention of sick pay entitlement. He applied to a tribunal for a declaration that such a term should be included.

Held: (CA) Although it may be possible for the court to imply a term concerning sick pay into a contract of employment, this should only be done if it is necessary for the long term maintenance of the employment relationship. However, it is open to the employer to produce evidence that the provision of sick pay was not the intention of the parties. [1982] I.C.R. 626.

Commentary
The later Court of Appeal decision in *Eagland v British Telecommunications plc* [1992] I.R.L.R. 323 goes further and makes it clear that the court should not imply terms into the contract of

employment if either there is evidence that such terms had been expressly omitted, or if there is no evidence that the term had been agreed.

It may appear that there is a potential conflict here between the inability in most instances of the court to introduce terms into the contract of employment, and the statutory duty of the court to determine, on occasions, what particulars ought to have been included in a section 1 statement (under s.11(1) of the Employment Rights Act 1996).

Key Principle: **At common law, the employer is under a duty to take reasonable care for the health and safety of his employees.**

Paris v Stepney Borough Council 1951

Mr Paris worked as a cleaner, part of his duties consisted of scraping rust from the underside of vehicles. It was not normal practice for the employer to provide goggles for this task. Mr Paris had only one good eye, and when a splinter of rust entered this eye, Mr Paris was totally blinded.

Held: (HL) The employer owes a duty of care not only to employees generally, but to each employee as an individual. Thus in the case of Mr Paris the employer should have foreseen there was a risk of greater injury and acted accordingly. [1951] 1 All E.R. 42.

Commentary

Although safety standards have been considerably increased through statute over the past 50 years, the principles in this case remain good. Thus if an employer is, or should be, aware that an employee is particularly vulnerable, they would have an increased duty of care towards that employee.

Key Principle: **The duty of mutual trust and confidence forms a fundamental term of every contract of employment.**

Woods v WM Carr Services (Peterborough) Ltd 1981

Ms Woods worked in a senior administrative role, but following a take-over she was required to take a cut in salary and work longer hours. When she refused to comply she was given additional duties and her job title was changed. She left claiming unfair dismissal.

Held: (EAT) "... it is clearly established that there is implied in a contract of employment a term that the employers will not, without reasonable and proper cause, conduct themselves in a manner calculated or likely to destroy or seriously damage the relationship of confidence and trust between employer and employee." *Per* Browne-Wilkinson J. [1981] I.C.R. 666.

Commentary

This has been approved in numerous subsequent decisions— although it is worth noting that in the case of *Woods* the EAT felt itself unable to interfere with the findings of the industrial tribunal that there was in this case no fundamental breach of contract by the employer.

United Bank Ltd v Akhtar 1989

Mr Akhtar had been employed by United Bank since 1978. His contract of employment contained a mobility clause, allowing the bank to move him at their discretion to any of their branches. In 1987 he was asked to move from Leeds to Birmingham, at short notice and with no financial assistance. For various reasons he refused and left claiming constructive and unfair dismissal.

Held: (EAT) Although the contract contained an express mobility clause, and the company were thus entitled to exercise their rights under that clause, the manner in which the company went about exercising their rights breached the implied term of mutual trust and confidence. Particularly in this case, the lack of notice period, the lack of financial assistance and the apparent refusal to consider Mr Akhtar's reasons for refusal. [1989] I.R.L.R. 507.

Commentary

On the one hand, an employer cannot be in breach of a specific term of the contract by exercising their rights under that term; however, if those rights are exercised in a manner so as to prevent the employee carrying out his part of the contract the employer will be in breach of the term of mutual trust and confidence. This is not to say that the employer must act "reasonably"—such a requirement would be contrary to the Court of Appeal reasoning in *Western Excavating v Sharp* [1978] Q.B. 761. On this issue, see also the case of *White v Reflecting Roadstuds Ltd* [1991] I.R.L.R. 331.

Malik v Bank of Credit and Commerce International 1997

Mr Malik was dismissed for redundancy when his employer, BCCI, went into liquidation. Mr Malik had worked for the bank for some 12 years, but because of the adverse publicity surrounding the collapse of the bank had found it very difficult to obtain suitable subsequent employment. He sought to bring a claim for damages based on a breach of the contract of employment by his employer, namely a breach of the term of mutual trust and confidence caused by the manner in which the bank had managed its affairs.

Held: (HL) It was accepted that the bank had operated in a corrupt and dishonest manner but that Mr Malik was innocent of any involvement, and it was further accepted that, following *Woods v WM Carr Services*, contracts of employment contain the implied term of mutual trust and confidence. The issue to be decided was, therefore, whether the manner in which the bank operated could breach that term in an employee's contract. Their Lordships were in no doubt that it could. Therefore Mr Malik's claim should succeed. [1997] I.R.L.R. 462.

Commentary
Thus the actions of the employer which constitute the breach of mutual trust and confidence need not be directed towards the employee.

Key Principle: **An employee has a duty to obey all reasonable and lawful orders.**

Laws v London Chronicle (Indicator Newspapers) Ltd 1959

Ms Laws worked in the advertising department of the newspaper. At a meeting which she attended, there was an argument between her immediate superior, the advertising manager, and the managing director. The advertising manager left the room instructing her to leave with him. The managing director ordered her to "stay where you are". She left with her line manager and was consequently dismissed for refusing to obey the managing director's order.

Held: (CA) The court held that wilful disobedience of a lawful and reasonable order indicated a complete disregard for an essential condition of the employment contract, and would justify a summary dismissal. However, due to the particular circumstances of this case, Ms Laws' actions did not amount to a fundamental breach of the contract. [1959] 1 W.L.R. 698.

Commentary

The court recognised that Ms Laws was in a "no win" situation. Had she complied with the managing director's instruction, it could be argued that trust and confidence between her manager and herself would have broken down.

Ottoman Bank v Chakarian 1930

Chakarian worked in an area controlled by the Turkish authorities, who some years previously had sentenced him to death. He requested that his employer transfer him out of the area. His employer refused and Chakarian fled the country, for which he was dismissed.

Held: (PC) Since there was a "grave risk to his person", Chakarian was not bound to obey the order to remain. [1930] A.C. 277.

Commentary

An old case, and decided on its somewhat extreme facts; but it has much potential relevance today. Presumably the "grave risk" may be brought about by violence, disease or other health related issues; thus locations of high violence levels, unsanitary conditions, or work causing stress related illness may be covered.

Key Principle: **The employee has a duty to adapt to new technology and working methods.**

Cresswell v Board of Inland Revenue 1984

Mrs Cresswell worked as a tax officer using a manual system of tax coding. The employer wished to computerise its operation and required that its employees should adapt. Mrs Cresswell, supported by her trade union, refused to comply, stating that the manual system had through custom and practice become a term of the employment contract.

Held: (ChD) The court held that the nature of the job had not fundamentally changed, and that employees, with proper training which the employer was obliged to provide, had therefore a duty to adapt to those changes. [1984] 2 All E.R. 713.

Commentary
Obviously, as technology progresses, businesses are expected to change their working methods so as to remain competitive; this inevitably requires employees to adapt to new methods and practices. *Cresswell* concerns an employee who would not adapt, the following case considers other aspects of the duty to adapt.

North Riding Garages v Butterwick 1967
Mr Butterwick had been employed for many years as a mechanic with a small garage, rising to the position of garage manager, but still spending much of his time as a "hands-on" mechanic. New owners required that he should spend much more of his time in a management and administrative role. He had considerable difficulty adapting to these changes, and was dismissed.

Held: (QBD) Holding that the nature of the work had not fundamentally changed, the court stated that "an employee who remains in the same kind of work is expected to adapt". *Per* Widgery J. [1967] 2 Q.B. 56.

Commentary
This case was actually brought because Mr Butterwick was claiming a redundancy payment, but it raises the issue of how extensive is the duty to adapt? In the case of *Cresswell* the employee refused to adapt, in the case of *Butterwick* it appears that the employee was unable to adapt. Lord Denning, in the case of *Hollister v National Union of Farmers* [1979] I.R.L.R. 238, was of the opinion that if the change was for sound business practice, a failure by the employee to adapt may give rise to a potentially fair reason for dismissal.

Key Principle: **There is no general right for an employer to unilaterally vary the terms of the employment contract.**

Burdett-Coutts v Hertfordshire County Council 1984
The plaintiffs were dinner ladies employed by the county council. Due to an alleged need to make financial savings, the

council, following unsuccessful negotiations with the trade union, wrote to the dinner ladies stating that in order to avoid redundancies it was necessary to make changes to various of the conditions of the employment contracts. The changes would result in a decrease in income to the employees. The employees continued to work as normal, not, they argued, because they accepted the contents of the letter, but because they were still employed under their original contracts and had not accepted any changes to those terms. The employer argued that the letter in fact terminated the contract of employment and offered a new contract on different terms and conditions, and by continuing to work, the employees were by implication accepting the new contract

Held: (QBD) The court refused to accept that the letter constituted termination of the original contract and offer of a new set of terms and conditions. They held that the letter was an attempt by the employer to unilaterally vary the terms and conditions of the existing contract, and, as such, amounted to a breach of contract by the employer. Furthermore, that by continuing to work, the employees had not indicated acceptance of the breach, but were merely working to the original contract. As such, the employees were entitled to recover the arrears of wages. [1984] I.R.L.R. 91.

Commentary
It is important to note that in this case the employees had made it clear that they would not accept the proposed changes. The outcome to such a case could well be very different if the employee does not make their objection known and continues to work—that could well amount to acceptance of the breach (the new terms) by action.

Jones v Associated Tunnelling Co Ltd 1981
From 1964 to 1969 Mr Jones was employed at a colliery site some two miles from his home. In 1969 his place of work was changed to another colliery some 12 miles from his home. In 1973 he was issued with a new statement of terms and conditions stating that this colliery was his place of work. A further statement of terms and conditions was issued in 1976, including a mobility clause obliging him if required to work at any other site. In 1980 the employer's contract at Mr Jones' place of work expired, and Mr Jones was offered further work at a different site at an equal distance from his home. Mr Jones chose not to

accept that work and left. He then claimed a redundancy payment from the employer. The employer argued that the inclusion of a mobility clause in the employment contract allowed them to move the employee as required, therefore they had not breached the contract and consequently there was no dismissal.

Held: (EAT) The EAT held that the right term to imply into Mr Jones' contract was that he could be required to work at any place within reasonable commuting distance from his home.

However, the EAT were not comfortable with the reasoning of the tribunal that by continuing to work without objection to the imposition of the mobility clause in 1976, Mr Jones had accepted the variation of his contract and was thus bound by the mobility clause. They suggested that where a worker was faced with a variation to the contract of employment, but that variation had no immediate practical application, and the worker continued to work without objection, the court should be careful before inferring that the worker was indicating acceptance of the variation. In such a situation, the court held, it would be unrealistic to expect the employee to risk a confrontation with the employer over a term which had no immediate practical impact. [1981] I.R.L.R. 477.

Commentary
On the one hand the EAT are content to imply a limited mobility clause into an employee's contract, but on the other hand, may not be prepared to uphold an express mobility clause if, at the time it is purported to be included into the contract, it has no immediate practical impact.

Key Principle: **There is no implied contractual term giving the employee the right to smoke at work.**

Dryden v Greater Glasgow Health Board 1992
Mrs Dryden had worked for some 15 years as a nursing auxiliary in the theatre section of the Western Infirmary in Glasgow. She generally smoked around 30 cigarettes per day. The nature of her job was such that she was unable to leave the building to smoke, but until 1991 areas were set aside in the

hospital in which smoking was permitted. In 1991, following the circulation of a consultative document, employees were advised of the implementation of a no-smoking policy throughout all hospitals in the region. Staff were offered advice and counselling both prior to and following the new policy. Shortly after the introduction of the ban Mrs Dryden left complaining of unfair dismissal through constructive dismissal. The tribunal found that there was no implied term in Mrs Dryden's contract entitling her to smoke at work.

Held: (EAT) The introduction of a no-smoking policy did not constitute a breach of the employee's contract, since there was no term either express or implied entitling her to smoke at work. The introduction of the no-smoking policy was merely a work rule, which the employer is entitled to make; failure by an employee to follow such a rule would amount to a breach of the duty to obey lawful orders. [1992] I.R.L.R. 469.

Commentary
The EAT does not appear to have fully addressed the question of whether a "smoking term" could have been introduced into Mrs Dryden's contract through custom and practice—she had, after all, smoked in the building with the full knowledge, and even assistance, for some 15 years. Obviously with an issue such as smoking, and particularly within a hospital environment, policy issues are of major importance.

Waltons & Morse v Dorrington 1997
Mrs Dorrington worked as a secretary for a firm of solicitors for some 11 years. For much of that time she worked in a well ventilated room with a number of others, some of whom smoked. In 1992 she was relocated to another part of the building which contained a number of heavy smokers and in which the air quality was poorer. Mrs Dorrington requested and attempted to move back to her original work area, but was refused. Feeling her health was being affected, Mrs Dorrington left her employment, and then brought a complaint of unfair dismissal through constructive dismissal.

Held: (EAT) The EAT upheld the findings of the tribunal that Mrs Dorrington had been constructively and unfairly dismissed. In particular, they affirmed that the employer has an implied duty to provide and monitor, so far as is reasonably practicable, a working environment in which it is reasonably suitable for his

employees to work; one method in which the employer could have fulfilled that duty would have been to prohibit smoking in the building. Furthermore, the tribunal found that the employer had not properly addressed Mrs Dorrington's complaint. [1997] I.R.L.R. 488.

Commentary
Whereas the case of *Dryden* specifically concerns contractual terms, this case is primarily a health and safety issue.

Key Principle: **Employees are under a wide-ranging duty of fidelity or good faith.**

Hivac Ltd v Park Royal Scientific Instruments Ltd 1946
Two of Hivac's employees worked part-time for Park Royal Scientific, a competitor. There was no evidence that the employees had passed on any confidential information to Park Royal, or indeed that they were in a position to do so. Hivac, however, applied for an injunction restraining Park Royal from employing them.

Held: (CA) In granting the injunction, the court sought to balance the opposing views; on the one hand, the right of a workman to spend his leisure time for profit if he wished, and on the other, the right of the employer to protect itself from its employees deliberately harming its business. [1946] Ch 169.

Commentary
It is thus clear that the duty of fidelity will prevent an employee working for a competitor during the existence of the contract of employment. After termination of the employment contract, such a situation would normally be dealt with by restraint of trade clauses (see Chapter 11). What, however, is the situation with part-time employees?

Robb v Green 1895
Green whilst still employed, copied lists of his employer's customers with a view to starting his own business.

Held: (CA) The duty of fidelity is such that an employee who seeks to canvass or make a list of his employer's customers may be restrained from doing so, regardless of whether there is an express term in the contract to that effect. [1895] 2 Q.B. 315.

Commentary
The employee has a duty to work for, not against, the employer. In the same way, an employee must account to his employer for any secret commissions he may make in the course of his employment (*Boston Deep Sea Fishing and Ice Co v Ansell* (1888) 39 ChD 339).

Ticehurst v British Telecommunications plc 1992
During industrial action consisting of a "work to rule", Mrs Ticehurst was asked to sign an agreement that she would work normally, otherwise she would not be allowed to work and would not be paid. Mrs Ticehurst refused to comply with her employer's request on that and subsequent days. At the end of the dispute Mrs Ticehurst claimed for lost wages. It was agreed that apart from her refusal to sign the undertaking, Mrs Ticehurst had done nothing that could constitute a breach of her employment contract.

Held: (CA) In order to breach the duty of faithful service or co-operation it was not necessary that the actions of the employee should actually have a detrimental effect on the business of the employer. It was sufficient that the employee's action was aimed or intended to cause disruption or inconvenience. Consequently, Mrs Ticehurst was in breach of her employment contract, and her claim for lost wages did not succeed. [1992] I.R.L.R. 219.

Commentary
Thus, it appears that it is not only the effect of the action of the employee that may breach the contract, but, if the effect of the action does not amount to a breach of the contract, the intention behind the action may do so.

One further issue in this case is that Mrs Ticehurst held a managerial post with BT, and it may perhaps be argued that the duty of fidelity is higher for managers than it may be for non-managerial employees?

Key Principle: **The employee is under a duty to account for secret profits.**

Boston Deep Sea Fishing & Ice Co v Ansell 1888
It was found that Ansell, the managing director of the company, had accepted commission from a shipbuilder for placing an order on behalf of the company for the construction of new vessels.

Held: (CA) "... if it is a profit which arises out of the transaction, it belongs to his master, and the agent or servant has no right to take it..." (1888) 39 ChD 339.

Commentary
Should the employee therefore make a secret profit from his employment he will be in breach of his contract of employment.

---

3. EQUAL PAY

The Relationship between European and UK legislation.

Key Principle: **National legislation must be construed in accord with European law.**

Defrenne v SABENA (No.2) 1976
Ms Defrenne worked as an air-hostess with SABENA. She claimed that the airline paid male stewards more than air-hostesses for doing exactly the same job. She brought her claim, not under national law, but under what is now Art.141. The first issue before the court was whether Art.141 had direct effect.

Held: (ECJ) Article 141 prohibits discrimination between men and women not only in respect of contracts between the individual and an emanation of the state, but also in employment contracts between individuals. [1976] I.C.R. 547.

Commentary
Thus it is possible to base a claim for equal pay on either national or European law.

Pickstone v Freemans plc 1988
Mrs Pickstone was employed as a warehouse operative by
Freemans, the mail-order company. She brought a claim for
equal pay, naming as a comparator a man working as a
"checker warehouse operative", claiming that her work was of
equal value to his, although he was paid more.

Held: (HL) In upholding Mrs Pickstone's claim, the House of
Lords addressed a number of important issues:

(a) National legislation should be construed in accord with
European law.

(b) An applicant is permitted to choose their own comparator, thus an employer is not able to circumvent the
legislation by the use of a "token male".

(c) An applicant will not be able to bring a claim for equal
pay under the head of "work of equal value" if a valid job
evaluation study is already in place. [1988] I.R.L.R. 357.

Commentary
This case is worth reading in full, as it addresses and may be used
as authority for a number of different issues. Regarding the
relationship between UK and European law, since national legislation must be construed in line with European law, it follows that a
national court will normally have no need to consider Art.141
because the EPA 1970 should provide an adequate remedy.

Although not an employment law issue specifically, it is worth
noting that this is one of the first cases in which an English court
referred to Hansard as an aid to construction—it predates the case
of *Pepper v Hart* by some five years.

Key Principle: **The limitation periods contained in s.2 of the
EPA 1970 have both been challenged as incompatible with EC
legislation.**

Levez v TH Jennings (Harlow Pools) Ltd 1999
The issue in this case was whether the two year limit on
backdating equal pay claims, contained in s.2(5) of the EPA
1970, was compatible with EC law. On reference to the ECJ it

was held that the two year limit did not infringe the principle of effectiveness; *i.e.* it did not make the provision of EC law impossible or unreasonably difficult to effect. On the question of equivalence (whether the two year limit was less favourable than other time limits in similar domestic legislation) the ECJ stated that it was for national courts to decide.

Held: (EAT) The two year limit imposed by the EPA was less favourable than limits imposed under contract for recovery of monies for unlawful deduction from wages and for unlawful discrimination in terms of employment on grounds of race or disability, which were legitimate comparisons. Therefore the six year limit under the Limitation Act should also apply to the EPA. [1999] I.R.L.R. 764.

Commentary
An important decision having considerable impact on many companies.

Preston v Wolverhampton Health Care NHS Trust 2000
In a test case, a number of part-time workers claimed retroactive membership of the NHS occupational pension scheme for periods of service prior to the time when amendments were introduced giving them equal rights to their full time colleagues. Two issues were raised: firstly, whether the two year limit on back-dating membership infringes the principle of effectiveness; and secondly, whether the six month time limit on the bringing of an action contravened the principle of effectiveness.

Held: (ECJ) The imposition of a two year limit on the back-dating of membership of the occupational pension scheme did infringe the principle of effectiveness, in as much as membership rights were guaranteed under EC law from at least the time of the *Defrenne* case, and a two year limit would disallow those employees from exercising those rights. Concerning the issue of the six month time limit, the ECJ held that, as long as the limit was no less favourable than other limits for similar actions under domestic law, the principle of equivalence would not be infringed. However, a domestic rule that the six month limit should start at the end of each contract, even in the case of workers who have worked on a series of consecutive contracts for the same employer, did infringe the principle of effectiveness. [2000] I.R.L.R. 506.

Commentary
Another important decision which allows many thousands of part-time workers retroactive membership of occupational pension schemes.

Heads of Claim

Key Principle: **Like Work. The term "like work" should be interpreted purposively.**

Capper Pass Ltd v Lawton 1977
Ms Lawton was employed as a cook in the directors' kitchen, generally providing lunch for between 10–20 persons per day. She claimed equality with two male assistant chefs working in the staff kitchens who were involved in the preparation of some 350 meals served in six sittings throughout the day. The issue for the court was whether the work done by Ms Lawton could be considered as "like work" with the work done by her comparators.

Held: (EAT) The court adopted a two-stage approach. First, asking whether the work done by the parties was the same or "broadly similar" in nature. If the work is broadly similar in nature, secondly, whether the differences between the work are of "practical importance in relation to terms and conditions of employment". Applying this approach, the court held that Ms Lawton's claim should succeed. [1977] I.C.R. 83.

Commentary
This use of the "broad brush" approach in defining "like work" has been approved in several Court of Appeal decisions. It is worth noting that at the time of this case, the first case of "like work" to be heard on appeal, the issue of "work of equal value" had not yet been enacted in UK law.

Shields v Coomes (Holdings) Ltd 1978
The employer was a bookmaker, having some 90 betting shops throughout the south of England. In most of those shops they employed two female counter staff. However, in nine of the

shops, in areas in which the company believed may be susceptible to trouble from customers, they employed one female and
one male. The male counterhand was paid more than the female
counterhand. One of the female counter staff brought an action
for equal pay. The company responded that male counter staff
were paid more because part of their job consisted of dealing
with trouble from customers when necessary, and that this
additional work warranted additional pay.

Held: (CA) Since in the previous three years there had not
actually been any trouble at the betting shops, there could not
be said to be any practical difference between the work done by
the men and the women. Thus Ms Shields claim should succeed.
[1978] I.C.R. 1159.

Commentary
This reconfirms that differences in pay between men and women
are, in such cases, only justifiable if there are real and practical
differences in the work they actually perform.

Macarthys Ltd v Smith 1980
Ms Smith was employed as a stockroom manager at a wage of
£50 per week. She discovered that her predecessor, a man, had
been paid £60 per week for doing an almost identical job. She
brought a claim for equal pay, naming her predecessor as
comparator.

Held: (ECJ) The main issue for the ECJ to consider was
whether Art.141 required the comparator to be a contemporary
of the applicant. The court confirmed that the principle of equal
pay did not depend upon both the applicant and the comparator
being employed at the same time. [1980] I.C.R. 672.

Commentary
Thus the case is authority for the proposition that the applicant
may compare themselves with their predecessor; it is also, on
occasion, possible for the complainant to use their successor as
comparator (see *Diocese of Hallam Trustee v Connaughton* [1996]
I.R.L.R. 505).

Key Principle: **Work Rated as Equivalent. The job evaluation
scheme must be objective.**

Rummler v Dato-Druck GmbH 1987

The job evaluation scheme adopted by the employer relied upon classifying jobs according to grading systems, one of which was the effort and exertion required by the employee. Mrs Rummler's job was graded as Grade II, requiring medium effort. She argued that the job should have been graded as Grade IV— requiring heavy effort—since for her the lifting of boxes weighing in excess of 20kgs amounted to heavy physical work.

Held: (ECJ) A job evaluation scheme will not necessarily be discriminatory merely because some of the criteria may be more easily met by one sex than the other. However, in so far as the nature of the job allows, the evaluation scheme must include other criteria which ensure that the scheme as a whole is not discriminatory. [1987] I.C.R. 774.

Commentary

On the one hand, equal work should result in equal pay—thus Mrs Rummler's claim should not succeed; on the other, if jobs are to be compared depending upon the amount of effort required, Mrs Rummler's claim should succeed.

This case was not brought under the UK head of "work rated as equivalent", but it demonstrates some of the problems encountered.

Key Principle: **Work of Equal Value. The head of "work of equal value" greatly increases the potential for equal pay claims.**

Hayward v Cammell Laird Shipbuilders Ltd 1988

Ms Hayward was employed as a cook. She claimed equal pay under the head of work of equal value with various tradesmen working in the shipyard. Her claim succeeded, but the employer argued that her overall remuneration package was at least equivalent to that of her comparators; she received paid meal breaks, longer holidays and enhanced sick pay scheme, which they did not—although their basic pay was higher than hers.

Held: (HL) The correct procedure under the legislation was to compare and equalise each individual component of the total pay package, not to consider the overall package in its entirety. [1988] I.C.R. 464.

Commentary
It is therefore then open to the comparators to bring a claim for equality and receive the same paid meal breaks, longer holidays and enhanced sick pay as Ms Hayward. This approach has since been confirmed by the ECJ in the case of *Barber v Guardian Royal Exchange* [1990] I.C.R. 616. Thus, the supposed dangers of "leap-frogging" by allowing terms to be equalised with the most favourable, does not constitute a valid defence.

Evesham v North Hertfordshire HA 2000
Ms Evesham, a speech therapist, brought a successful claim under the head of work of equal value, naming as her comparator a male clinical psychologist. A remedies hearing was held to determine how her contract should be modified under the EPA 1970 to ensure that her terms were not less favourable than those of her comparator. At the time of the original claim, Ms Evesham had held her post for six years, whereas her comparator was in his first year. She argued that, since both posts carried annual increments, she should not be placed on the same level as her comparator, but should be on a level indicating her six years' experience.

Held: (CA) Her appeal was dismissed. The EPA 1970 only requires that a successful applicant should be treated equally to the comparator chosen. If she were to enter the pay scale at a level higher than her comparator, she would, in effect, be getting parity with someone with whom she had not established an equal value claim. [2000] I.R.L.R. 257.

Commentary
The case reinforces the importance of choosing as a comparator someone of equal standing, not only in terms of work done, but also regarding seniority, etc.

Key Principle: **If the chosen comparator works at a different location to the claimant, it is necessary that "common terms and conditions" apply.**

British Coal Corp. v Smith 1996
Over 1,000 women employed as canteen workers and cleaners at almost 50 different sites throughout the UK claimed equal pay on the basis of work of equal value with 150 male surface workers and clerical staff at 14 different establishments. The company argued that common terms and conditions did not apply across the establishments, and consequently the claims should not succeed.

Held: (HL) The House of Lords questioned what was meant by the phrase "common terms and conditions". Either it meant that there should be no differences, other than *de minimis* exceptions, in which case the women were almost bound to fail at the first hurdle; or it meant that the terms and conditions had to be sufficiently similar for a fair comparison to be made. Their Lordships held that, in their opinion, parliament could not have intended that terms and conditions should be identical, but rather that they should be substantially comparable on a broad basis. On that understanding, the findings of the tribunal that the women were employed in the same employment was upheld. [1996] I.R.L.R. 404.

Commentary
Thus the broad approach of the House of Lords in the earlier case of *Leverton v Clwyd County Council* [1989] I.R.L.R. 28 was continued.

South Ayrshire Council v Morton 2002
Ms Morton was a primary school teacher and along with two colleagues brought a claim for equal pay under the Equal Pay Directive, arising under Art.141, naming male secondary school teachers as comparators. Two of the comparators worked for the same Local Education Authority (LEA) as Ms Morton and her colleagues, the third worked for a different LEA. The employer argued that the use of a comparator from a different LEA was not lawful.

Held: (CS) Distinguishing actions brought under the EPA 1970, which restricts the choice of comparators to those working for the same or associated employers, Art.141 should in this particular instance be interpreted to include all those LEAs operating under the same collective agreement. [2002] I.R.L.R. 256.

Commentary
A potentially important decision, in that it may serve to extend the scope of comparison; although the court did, in effect, restrict itself to the particular facts of this case.

Key Principle: **In a claim of work of equal value, even if the complaint is referred by the tribunal to an independent expert, the tribunal are not obliged to follow the expert's recommendation.**

Tennants Textile Colours Ltd v Todd 1989
The importance of this case lies in the ruling made by the tribunal that once the independent expert's report had been admitted as evidence its findings should be binding as fact on the parties.

Held: (CA) The independent expert's report is not binding on the parties. An independent expert's report must be obtained unless it is clear to the tribunal that the claimant could not win, and unless for one of three specific reasons the tribunal decides that the report should not be received, it must be admitted as evidence. However, the tribunal is not bound to follow the report either in part or in whole. [1989] I.R.L.R. 3.

Commentary
Thus, the independent expert's report forms an important part of the evidence available to the tribunal—but it is open to the tribunal to either accept or reject it.

Scope of the Legislation

Key Principle: **The EPA 1970 is concerned with discrimination on the grounds of gender, and not with fairness.**

Glasgow City Council v Marshall 2000
The applicants were seven female and one male instructors working in special schools in Scotland. Teachers working in the same schools were paid more than the instructors. It was

accepted that although the teachers had higher qualifications than the instructors, both groups performed the same or similar work. The female instructors named a male teacher as comparator, and the male instructor named a female teacher.

Held: (HL) The defence put forward by the employer succeeded. They claimed that the difference in pay was due to collective agreements, and further, that the differences did not discriminate on the grounds of sex—95 per cent of both the instructors and the teachers were female. Lord Slynn stated: "This is plainly in essence a claim that the pay is not fair; and not a claim that the pay is unequal because of discrimination between the sexes. As such, it does not fall within the Equal Pay Act 1970." [2000] I.R.L.R. 272.

Commentary
It is therefore clear that, despite earlier case law which may indicate otherwise, it is not possible to succeed in an equal pay claim merely because the applicant is able to point to a comparator of the opposite sex and show that the work undertaken by both is the same or similar. An employer's defence under s.1(3) of the EPA 1970 will defeat such a claim if four stages are satisfied: First, that the explanation for the pay variance is genuine. Second, that the less favourable treatment is a result of that reason. Third, that the reason is not the difference of sex, whether amounting to either direct or indirect discrimination. Fourth, that the factor relied upon is (or in the case of a s.1(3)(b) claim—since the wording is different—may be) a material difference between the woman's case and the man's case.

Defences

Key Principle: **Section 1(3) of the EPA 1970 provides for the defence of "genuine material factor".**

Eaton Ltd v Nuttall 1977
The applicant was one of a number of production schedulers, responsible for ordering and scheduling materials. She claimed equal pay on the basis of like work with a male production scheduler who was paid more than her. The applicant looked

after 2,400 items with a value up to £2.50, her comparator looked after 1,200 items with values between £5.00 and £1,000.

Held: (EAT) The difference in value of the various items amounted to a genuine material factor allowing for the differential in pay. The court held that, although the work done by both was in many ways identical, due to the difference in value of the items, an error by the comparator was likely to have much more serious consequences than an error by the applicant. [1977] I.R.L.R. 71.

Commentary
Thus, level of responsibility or consequence of mistake may amount to a defence to an equal pay claim.

Snoxell v Vauxhall Motors Ltd 1977
Prior to the implementation of the EPA 1970, the company had operated different pay scales for men and women. In 1971 an amended structure was introduced including both women and men. It was accepted that one previously male grade had in the past been rated and paid too highly, and although under the new structure those in this grade were down-graded, their salary level was maintained by means of "red-circling". Two women of a similar grade claimed equal pay with their "red-circled" colleagues, arguing that the only reason they were not paid at a similar level was that, being women, prior to 1971 they had not been eligible for inclusion in that grade.

Held: (EAT) Although "red-circling" may amount to a genuine material factor defence, in this case the defence should fail, since the differential in pay was brought about by reason of the sex of the workers. [1977] I.R.L.R. 123.

Commentary
It is therefore important to determine why the original pay difference has come about; if through reasons of sex discrimination, then the defence should not succeed.

Key Principle: **The scope of the defence of "market forces" has been restricted by the courts.**

Enderby v Frenchay HA 1994
Dr Enderby, a speech therapist, brought a claim under work of equal value with male pharmacists and clinical psychologists all employed by the NHS. Dr Enderby appealed against the finding of the tribunal arguing that she had established a *prima facie* case of indirect discrimination in that she was a member of a predominantly female group, doing work of equal value as, but being paid less than, a group of predominantly male employees. The employer argued that any difference in pay structure was due to market forces, and thus a valid defence under s.1(3) of the EPA 1970.

Held: (ECJ) It is for the national court to determine what proportion of the pay differential is due to genuine objective market forces. Only this part of any differential may be justified under Community law. [1994] I.C.R. 112.

Commentary
This decision restricts the view of market forces taken in the earlier case of *Rainey v Greater Glasgow Health Board* [1987] I.C.R. 129, and was applied in the later case of *Ratcliffe v North Yorkshire County Council* [1995] I.R.L.R. 439.

The defence of market forces therefore continues to be available, but will be applied strictly by the courts, and will only be available for as long as the particular set of circumstances apply.

---

4. DISCRIMINATION

Sex and Race Discrimination

Scope of the Legislation

Key Principle: **For the purpose of the Race Relations Act 1976, the courts have laid down a test to determine the meaning of "ethnic origin".**

Mandla v Dowell Lee 1983
A Sikh boy was refused admission to a private school for failure to comply with dress regulations. The first issue for the court

was whether Sikhs qualified as a racial or ethnic group within the meaning of the RRA.

Held: (HL) There are two conditions which must be satisfied for any group to be included under the RRA:

(a) a long shared history, of which the group is conscious as distinguishing itself from other groups, and the memory of which it keeps alive, and

(b) a cultural tradition of its own, including family and social customs and manners, often but not necessarily associated with religious observance.

Additionally, the court found four other conditions to be of importance, but not necessarily essential:

(c) a common geographical origin or descent from a small number of common ancestors,

(d) a common language, that need not be different from neighbouring or surrounding groups,

(e) a common religion, different from neighbouring or surrounding groups,

(f) being a minority or oppressed or dominant group within a community.

Thus it was held that Sikhs are an ethnic group. [1983] I.C.R. 385.

Commentary
Applying these conditions, it has since been shown that, for the purposes of the RRA, Jews and Romanies (the original case law uses the term "Gypsies" rather than "Romanies") are ethnic groups, whereas Jehovah's Witnesses and Rastafarians are not (but bear in mind now legislation concerning discrimination on religious grounds).

Key Principle: **The phrase "can comply" in s.1(1)(b)(i) of the RRA has been purposively defined by the courts.**

Mandla v Dowell Lee 1983
A Sikh boy was allowed admittance to an independent school on condition that he wore the full school uniform, including a

cap. It was argued that he could not comply with that requirement, since his religion required him to wear a turban. Since it
was theoretically possible for him to remove his turban and
wear a cap, the court needed to define the phrase "can comply".

Held: (HL) If the word "can" is taken literally, it would mean
that Sikhs and members of other racial or ethnic groups would
be deprived of the protection Parliament obviously intended the
RRA to afford them. Thus "can comply" must be read as "can
in practice comply". [1983] I.C.R. 385.

Commentary
The fact that some Sikhs may choose to comply with a "no
turban" rule is irrelevant. The court held that "can in practice"
had the meaning of "can consistently with the customs and
cultural conditions of the racial group".

Key Principle: **Positive discrimination is generally unlawful.**

Jepson and Dyas-Elliot v The Labour Party 1996
In an apparent effort to increase the number of female Members
of Parliament in order to promote equality, the Labour Party
sought to restrict selection lists in several constituencies to
women only.

Held: (IT) Since discrimination in favour of one group
amounts to discrimination against another group, positive discrimination in favour of women is unlawful. [1996] I.R.L.R. 116.

Commentary
It is necessary to differentiate between positive action—
encouraging members of under-represented groups to apply for
positions, promotion or training—which is lawful, and positive
discrimination, which generally is not.

Marschall v Land Nordrhein Westfalen 1998
Mr Marschall was a teacher employed in a state school. The
education authority operated a rule under which if there were
fewer women than men in the higher grade level, women were
to be given priority for promotion to that grade assuming that
their candidature was at least comparable to that of the male

applicant. Mr Marschall challenged that rule, and the case went before the ECJ.

Held: (ECJ) Article 2(4) of Directive 76/207—the Equal Treatment Directive—allows for measures to promote equal opportunities for men and women by removing any existing inequalities. Thus, it is argued, if positive discrimination does nothing more than redress the effects of past discrimination, it is permissible under Art.2(4).

The court held that the Equal Treatment Directive would not be breached if there is a guarantee that all candidates will be subject to an objective assessment which takes into account all the factors specific to the individual candidate, and the criteria used in the assessment are not in themselves discriminatory. [1998] I.R.L.R. 39.

Commentary
It is very difficult to determine the scope of this judgment, but it may indicate a more pragmatic approach from the ECJ towards the issue of positive discrimination. It should also be remembered that there are provisions within the Treaty of Amsterdam to permit member states to adopt measures which provide for "specific advantages" to an under-represented sex in order to achieve full equality. Such measures must in themselves amount to positive discrimination.

Re: Badeck's Application 2000
Officers of the local government of the region of Hesse sought to challenge the legality of a Hesse law introduced for the purpose of providing equal access for women and men to public sector positions by giving preference on the basis of sex in those cases where a particular sex was under-represented.

Held: (ECJ) It was not unlawful to give preference to women in those areas in which they were under-represented, as the purpose of Council Directive 76/207 was to introduce equality by removing imbalances. However, it was important that such measures did not give automatic priority to women over equally qualified men. [2000] I.R.L.R. 432.

Commentary
It would appear, however, that in the case of two equally qualified applicants, one male and one female, for a public sector post in an

area in which women were under-represented, failure to give priority to the woman may lead to a claim of sex discrimination.

Key Principle: **Previously, sex discrimination legislation has not covered discrimination on the grounds of sexual orientation; however from December 2003 legislation (SI 2003/1661— The Employment Equality (Sexual Orientation) Regulations 2003) is in place giving effect to the EC Directive on Discrimination and amending the Sex Discrimination Act 1975 to include sexual orientation.**

Smith v Gardner Merchant Ltd 1998

Mr Smith, a male homosexual, was dismissed from his job following complaints by a female member of staff. Smith alleged that he had been sexually harassed by reason of his sexual orientation, by the female member of staff, and that such treatment was contrary to the Sex Discrimination Act 1975.

Held: (CA) The court agreed that Mr Smith had been sexually harassed by reason of his sexual orientation, but held that sexual orientation was not covered by the Sex Discrimination Act, sexual orientation not being an aspect of the person's sex or gender. However, in this particular case, Mr Smith had been treated less favourably than a homosexual woman would have been, and thus a case of sex discrimination could be proven. [1998] I.R.L.R. 510.

Commentary

This, along with the following, case is now of historical interest only; but it demonstrates the problems faced by some employees previously.

Grant v South-West Trains Ltd 1998

Ms Grant was employed by South-West Trains, included in her contract of employment was a clause which allowed both her and her spouse and dependants travel concessions. Further company rules defined "spouse" as either legal spouse or common law spouse of the opposite sex. Ms Grant's request for travel concessions for her partner was refused on the grounds that her partner was not of the opposite sex. She argued that this refusal was contrary to EC law.

Held: (ECJ) The conditions laid down by the company provide for travel concessions for staff and their spouse of the opposite sex. Since they do not discriminate on the basis of the sex of the employee (in that a male employee with a same sex partner would be treated in the same way as a female employee with a same sex partner), the restriction cannot constitute discrimination directly based on sex. [1998] I.R.L.R. 206.

Commentary
Provision had been made in the Treaty of Amsterdam for discrimination law to be extended to cover sexual orientation, but at the time of this case this had not taken place. When the case came before the House of Lords (2003), the findings of the ECJ were followed. See also the case of *Advocate General for Scotland v MacDonald* [2003] S.L.T. 1158, in which both the House of Lords and the Court of Sessions held that sexual orientation was not at that time covered by the Sex Discrimination Act 1975 despite a strong argument to the contrary by the EAT.

Key Principle: **The motive behind the discriminatory action is irrelevant.**

James v Eastleigh Borough Council 1990
Eastleigh Borough Council introduced a scheme whereby pensioners were able to use the municipal swimming pool free of charge, other citizens had to pay an admission charge. This had the effect of allowing women free swimming from the age of 60, whereas men were not entitled until the age of 65. Mr James who was 61 claimed that since his wife who was also 61 was allowed free swimming, the council were discriminating against him on the grounds of his sex by not affording him the same facility.

Held: (HL) In a majority (3:2) decision, the court held that the motive for the discrimination was irrelevant; either the action complained of was discriminatory, or it was not. It posed the question: "Would the plaintiff, a man of 61, have received the same treatment as his wife but for his sex?" Answering in the affirmative, it followed that a case of direct discrimination had been proven. [1990] I.R.L.R. 288.

Commentary
Thus even the best intentioned motive may give rise to unlawful discrimination—but see also, the issue of positive discrimination

and the issues raised by the case of *Advocate General for Scotland v MacDonald* [2003] S.L.T. 1158.

Key Principle: **Discrimination "on racial grounds" may cover discrimination aimed at a third party.**

Weathersfield Ltd (t/a Van & Truck Rentals) v Sargent 1999
Mrs Sargent, of white European background, obtained a position as receptionist with the company. During training, she was told that the company had a special policy regarding ethnic minority customers: should any black or Asian customers telephone, she should tell them that no vehicles were available. Later, a director of the company confirmed the company policy to her. Mrs Sargent decided she could not work to such a policy and left, although at the time she did not give her reasons. She then brought a complaint of race discrimination.

Held: (CA) The tribunal were right to give a broad meaning to the expression "racial grounds" and holding that Mrs Sargent had been unfavourably treated on racial grounds by being required to carry out a racially discriminatory policy, even though she herself did not belong to the racial or ethnic group against whom the policy was aimed. [1999] I.R.L.R. 94.

Commentary
It is therefore possible to bring a successful action under the RRA if the complainant is treated unfavourably because of another person's race.

Harassment

Key Principle: **Harassment consists of any unwanted physical or verbal conduct directed against an individual on account of his or her sex or race. Racial harassment is specifically dealt with under the Race Relations Act 1976 (Amendment) Regulations 2003, which came into force July 19, 2003.**

Porcelli v Strathclyde Regional Council 1986
Mrs Porcelli worked as a laboratory technician, alongside two other technicians, both men. The two other technicians carried out a policy of unpleasantness against her, consisting of both sexual and non-sexual aggressive words and actions. She brought a claim of sexual harassment against her employer on the basis that they had vicarious liability for the actions of their employees. The employer defended the case arguing that the words and actions directed against Mrs Porcelli were similar and no worse than actions which would have been taken against an equally disliked male worker.

Held: (CS) The fact that an equally disliked male member of staff may have been treated in an equally unpleasant manner was not relevant. The fact that some, indeed most, of the action taken against Mrs Porcelli was gender specific was sufficient to prove sexual harassment. [1986] I.R.L.R. 134.

Commentary
The purpose of the action taken against Mrs Porcelli was apparently to make her unhappy with a view to forcing her resignation, and, argued the Court of Sessions, whilst it may be true that equally unpleasant action may have been taken against a male worker, the actual acts undertaken and words spoken would doubtless have been different. The CS therefore held that the actual treatment of Mrs Porcelli was on account of her sex.

This issue was re-examined by the House of Lords in the case of *Advocate General for Scotland v MacDonald* [2003] S.L.T. 1158, who disapproved the argument in *Porcelli*, stating that it widened the scope for sexual harassment to include cases where the motive of the harasser was not sexual—and thus casting doubt on the argument that the motive for discrimination is irrelevant. It was further argued by their Lordships that to follow *Porcelli* would mean that if a man is subjected to cruel treatment that is not gender specific, and a woman is subjected to less cruel treatment which is gender specific, the treatment of the woman and the man could not be compared in terms of the issue of "less favourable treatment". The case of *Porcelli* was thus disapproved, and should therefore no longer be followed.

Bracebridge Engineering Ltd v Darby 1990
Mrs Darby whilst at work was indecently assaulted by both her supervisor and her manager. The following day she complained

to the general manager, but as both of the perpetrators denied the incident, no further action was taken. She then left, claiming both unfair dismissal through constructive dismissal, and sexual harassment. Regarding the issue of sexual harassment, two issues of importance were considered.

Held: (EAT) Actions amounting to harassment do not necessarily take the employees committing those actions outside the course of employment; thus, the employer will still have vicarious liability for the actions of his employees whilst in the course of their employment. Secondly, although harassment normally consists of a course of either spoken or physical conduct, if the act is sufficiently serious, a single physical act may constitute harassment. [1990] I.R.L.R. 3.

Commentary
Earlier definitions of harassment spoke of a course of action, rather than a single act.

In Situ Cleaning Co Ltd v Heads 1995
Mrs Heads worked as a supervisor for In Situ Cleaning. One of the managers, Michael Brown, was the son of two of the company directors, and almost half the age of Mrs Heads. On one occasion he addressed her with the words: "Hiya, big tits". Mrs Heads complained to her employers, but Brown denied the incident. One of the issues before the court was whether a single spoken comment could amount to harassment.

Held: "Whether a single act of verbal sexual harassment is sufficient to found a complaint is ... a question of fact and degree." In this case the court held that it could. [1995] I.R.L.R. 4.

Commentary
Thus, it is clear that, if sufficiently serious, a single spoken comment—which in this case, it is claimed, was not overheard by any third party—may amount to sexual harassment. The case also raised other issues. Part of the employer's argument was that the remark was not sex-related, in that a similar comment could have been made to a man, for example relating to a beard or bald head. The court dismissed such an argument as absurd, stating that a remark by a man about a woman's breasts cannot sensibly be equated with a remark by a woman about a bald head or a beard. "One is sexual the other is not." Although this is palpably true, it

should be remembered that sexual harassment is considered as direct discrimination under the Sex Discrimination Act 1975 which deals with treatment on the basis of gender. May it therefore be argued that since a woman's breasts are gender specific, so is a man's beard or bald head?

The final point is that the court also made clear that any complaint of sexual harassment should be dealt with from the perception of the person aggrieved.

Driskel v Peninsula Business Services Ltd 2000
Ms Driskel complained to a tribunal of sex discrimination following a series of comments made to her over a period of time by her manager. Her complaint was dismissed on the grounds that none of the comments by themselves were sufficient to constitute sex discrimination, they had not been intended to be offensive, and she had not complained at the time to her employer.

Held: (EAT) Her appeal succeeded. The tribunal should have considered the comments as a whole in deciding whether they amounted to sex discrimination. Furthermore, comments or actions should be viewed subjectively, from the recipient's point of view, in deciding whether they amounted to sex discrimination. [2000] I.R.L.R. 151.

Commentary
Thus, if the comments directed to a woman are such as would not have been made to a man (or *vice versa*), and had the effect of undermining her dignity or otherwise disadvantaging her, they may amount to sex discrimination.

Victimisation

Key Principle: **It is not necessary to prove "conscious motivation" on the part of the alleged victimiser in order to prove victimisation.**

Nagarajan v London Regional Transport 1999
Between 1979 and 1989 Mr Nagarajan had worked in various capacities for different divisions of London Regional Transport.

During that time he had brought several cases alleging racial discrimination and victimisation, some of which were successful, some of which were not. Following a period of unemployment, Mr Nagarajan applied for a post with London Regional Transport, for which he was interviewed but found unsuitable. He brought proceedings alleging victimisation.

Held: (HL) The employment tribunal found as a question of fact that the decision of the interviewers had been "consciously or unconsciously" influenced by Mr Nagarajan's previous dealings with the employer. This was reversed by the Court of Appeal who stated that in order to satisfy s.2(1) of the RRA 1976 the discriminator must have a conscious motive connected with the legislation. The House of Lords, however, in restoring the findings of the employment tribunal, held that the question to be asked was simply: "Why did the defendant treat the employee less favourably?" It was not necessary to attempt to distinguish between conscious and subconscious motivation. [1999] I.R.L.R. 572.

Commentary
This case doubts the *obiter dicta* in *Aziz v Trinity Street Taxis Ltd* [1988] I.C.R. 534, which suggests that conscious motivation must be proven.

Indirect Discrimination

Key Principle: **Indirect Discrimination is the applying of a requirement or condition to all employees or potential employees, but the proportion of any particular sex or race who can comply with the condition is considerably smaller than the proportion of those from outside that sex or race who can comply, and the employer cannot justify that requirement, and the complainant's inability to comply with the requirement is to their detriment.**

R v Secretary of State for Employment *ex p.* EOC 1994
The Equal Opportunities Commission brought an action arguing that the hours threshold required under existing legislation for part-time employees to claim for redundancy pay and unfair

dismissal compensation constituted unlawful sex discrimination. They argued that since some 90 per cent of part-time employees working less than the required 16 hours per week were women, the legislation had the effect of indirectly discriminating against women.

Held: (HL) The hours threshold did constitute indirect sex discrimination, and the threshold was not capable of objective justification. [1995] 1 A.C. 1.

Commentary
Following this decision, the Government introduced the Employment Protection (Part-time Employees) Regulations 1995, which had the effect of removing the hours threshold completely. For a further example of the scope of indirect sex discrimination see the case of *R v Secretary of State for Employment ex p. Seymour-Smith* (Case C–167/97) ECJ.

Price v Civil Service Commission 1978
Ms Price applied for a post within the Civil service. The job specification stated that applicants should be between 17–28 years of age. At the time she was 35. She argued that the age restriction amounted to indirect sex discrimination against women, since many women between those ages were looking after children and thus out of the job market.

Held: (EAT) The court acknowledged that many women between the mid-twenties to the mid-thirties were engaged in bearing or minding children, and it therefore followed that those women would find it more difficult, if not impossible to comply with the age requirement. The further question to be addressed was whether the number of women who could comply with the requirement amounted to a "considerably smaller" proportion than the proportion of men who could comply—as required by the legislation. This required the court to consider the correct "pool" of applicants for comparison. The court held that the correct pool for comparison was the pool of potential applicants, rather than the pool of actual applicants. On these findings Ms Price's case should succeed. [1978] I.C.R. 27.

Commentary
The issue of "pool of comparators" has given the courts problems in the past. Had the correct pool in *Price's* Case been the pool of

actual applicants, statistics would have showed that a virtually equal percentage of women and men had been recruited. However, the pool of potential applicants contained not only those who applied, but also those who did not apply due to the age requirement. This issue has been further addressed by the Court of Appeal in the following case.

Jones v University of Manchester 1993
The university advertised for "a graduate, preferably aged between 27–35 with a record of successful experience in an industrial, commercial or public service setting". Miss Jones, who was 46 years of age and had obtained her degree as a mature student when aged 38, applied for the post for which she was otherwise well qualified, but was not short-listed, apparently due to her age. She complained of unlawful sex discrimination. As a case of indirect discrimination it fell to the court to identify the correct pool of comparators. At first instance it was held that the correct pool was the total of those graduates who graduated after the age of 25—mature students—and in this pool were a considerably smaller proportion of women than of men.

Held: (CA) The relevant pool should consist of all graduates, since the position advertised was open to all of those with a degree, not just to mature students. On this basis the proportion of women who could comply was much closer to the proportion of men. [1993] I.C.R. 474.

Commentary
Therefore the pool of comparators should consist of all of those to whom the condition applies. Bear in mind that in this case the condition was not mandatory, if it had been the argument in *Price* would have been relevant.

Key Principle: **When considering s.1(1)(b) of the RRA 1976 or s.1(1)(b) of the SDA 1975, it is necessary to define what is meant by "a requirement or condition".**

Perera v The Civil Service Commission 1983
Mr Perera, a Sri Lankan by birth, had qualified and practiced as a lawyer in that country. He had also been called to the Bar in

the UK. He had lived in the UK since 1973 and was employed by the Civil Service as an executive officer. On a number of occasions he had been unsuccessful in either transferring to the Civil Service legal service, or of achieving promotion. He brought a complaint of racial discrimination following his rejection for a post as legal assistant.

Held: (CA) As a first step, it must be shown that the Civil Service Commission had applied a requirement or condition to the post. The only requirement or condition applied had been that the successful applicant should be a barrister or solicitor; other factors taken into account were experience in the UK, command of English, nationality, and age—but the court held that these were not essential requirements, and, as such, could not be termed "requirements or conditions". Consequently, Mr Perera's action must fail. [1983] I.R.L.R. 166.

Commentary
This approach indicates a very strict interpretation of "requirement or condition" as being an absolutely essential factor. It is suggested that the more liberal approach in the following case is more in line with the European purposive approach, and is to be preferred.

Falkirk Council v Whyte 1997
Ms Whyte had applied for a managerial post within a prison run by Falkirk Council. Her application had been unsuccessful and she complained that the Council had indirectly discriminated against her by applying a requirement or condition which was such that the proportion of women who could comply with it was considerably smaller than the proportion of men who could comply—s.1(1)(b) of the SDA 1975. The requirement or condition was the need for management and supervisory experience.

The tribunal found in favour of Ms Whyte, but the Council appealed on the grounds that the issue of management and supervisory experience was not an absolute essential, and thus could not be a "requirement or condition".

Held: (EAT) The tribunal were entitled to apply a liberal interpretation to the words "requirement or condition", and the earlier case of *Perera* was disapproved. [1997] I.R.L.R. 560.

Commentary
Although the issue of management and supervisory experience was said by the Council to be only a desirable factor, the court found that it was a decisive factor in the selection procedure.

Dress Codes

Key Principle: **Dress codes will not normally constitute unlawful discrimination if they apply similar standards of conventionality to both men and women.**

Smith v Safeway plc 1996
Mr Smith was dismissed for wearing his hair long and in a pony-tail. The employer's dress code stated that men should have tidy hair, not below shirt collar length, and women with shoulder-length hair should have it tied or clipped back. Mr Smith complained of sex discrimination, and initially his claim was successful.

Held: (CA) The court held that different dress codes for men and women were lawful as long as the employer applied conventional standards to both sexes. [1996] I.R.L.R. 456.

Commentary
Be aware, however, of such cases as the PGA ban on female employees wearing trousers, which resulted in an out-of-court settlement of some £50,000 following a claim for unfair dismissal and sex discrimination.

It is very possible that some dress codes or personal appearance issues may fall foul of the Human Rights Act 1998.

Key Principle: **Dress codes may also give rise to complaints of racial discrimination.**

Singh v Rowntree Mackintosh 1979
The employer operated a policy of "no beards" for those employees engaged in food preparation or handling. This policy amounted to indirect discrimination against Sikhs.

Held: (EAT) Such a policy was justifiable in the interests of food hygiene. [1979] I.R.L.R. 199.

Kaur v Butcher & Baker Foods Ltd 1997

Mrs Kaur was dismissed for carrying a dagger at work, in contravention of the company's rules on the wearing of jewellery in food preparation areas. Mrs Kaur, a Sikh, argued that the dagger was one of the five K's required by the Sikh religion to be carried at all times.

Held: (ET) The tribunal upheld Mrs Kaur's complaint, making a finding of unlawful race discrimination against the employer. Case 1304563/97.

Commentary

Although the case of *Kaur* is only an Employment Tribunal decision, it is perhaps indicative of a move away from the approach of the courts in *Singh*, although firm authority on this area of law is presently awaited.

Vicarious Liability

Key Principle: **In respect of discrimination cases, the definition of "in the course of employment" is wider than the standard tortious definition.**

Jones v Tower Boot Co Ltd 1997

Jones was a 16 year old of mixed race. He started work at the Tower Boot Company in 1992, a company which apparently had not previously employed anyone from an ethnic minority. Jones was subjected to a campaign of racial abuse and harassment, consisting of name calling, "practical jokes" and physical abuse—including having his legs whipped with a piece of welt, having metal bolts thrown at his head and having his arm burned with a hot screwdriver. After a month of such treatment Jones left and brought a claim of racial discrimination, claiming that his fellow employees had subjected him to racial harassment for which the employer was vicariously liable.

At first instance, the tribunal found as a question of fact that Mr Jones had been subjected to racial harassment, and, further, that the harassment had been "done by a person in the course of his employment". On appeal however, the EAT held that they were bound by the authority of such cases as *Irving v The Post Office* [1987] I.R.L.R. 289 to apply the tortious test—in effect, was the act complained of carried out as part of the job which the perpetrator was employed to perform? The obvious answer to this question was "no"—of course the perpetrator was not employed to carry out acts of racial discrimination, thus the employer escaped liability. With the backing of the Commission for Racial Equality an appeal was taken to the Court of Appeal to challenge the meaning of the words "in the course of employment".

Held: (CA) The court adopted a purposive approach, accepting that it would be wrong to allow instances of racial (and presumably also sexual) harassment to "slip through the net of employer responsibility" by applying a common law principle evolved to deal with wrongdoings of a very different kind. The court held that it was open to, and indeed required of, a tribunal to interpret ordinary words in the sense which the layman would understand. The court therefore held that the order of the industrial tribunal should be restored. [1997] I.R.L.R. 168.

Commentary
Thus the phrase "in the course of employment" should be interpreted in the way a layman would understand it, and the narrower tortious meaning would not therefore apply to cases of discrimination.

Chief Constable of the Lincolnshire Police v Stubbs 1999
Detective Constable Deborah Stubbs was a member of the Lincolnshire Constabulary, on secondment to the Regional Crime Squad. She claimed that on two occasions she was subjected to sexual harassment by a Detective Sergeant Walker, also a member of Lincolnshire Constabulary on secondment to the Regional Crime Squad. The first occasion was after her turn of duty, at a pub where there were a number of other police officers; the second occasion was at a leaving party, which she attended with her boyfriend. One of the issues to be addressed was whether the incidents took place "in the course of employment", and thus whether the employer was vicariously liable.

Held: (EAT) Following the judgment in *Jones v Tower Boot Co Ltd* the term "in the course of employment" should be interpreted in lay terms, and although each case should be decided on its facts, it was open to a tribunal to find that a social gathering of work colleagues fell within that definition. [1999] I.R.L.R. 81.

Commentary
It is more likely that a leaving party will fall within the definition, rather than a mere gathering of work colleagues "after work".

It was later held, in the case of *Chief Constable of Bedfordshire Police v Liversidge* (2002) E.C.W.A. Civ. 894, that claims for race discrimination could, in most circumstances, not be brought against a chief constable, and thus arguably neither could a complaint of sex discrimination—case law under the two forms of discrimination being virtually interchangeable—however, in the case of *Chief Constable of Kent v Baskerville* (EAT 9/7/03) it was explained that since the Equal Treatment Directive 76/207/EEC impacted upon issues of sex discrimination but not race discrimination, therefore a different outcome may be produced.

Key Principle: **The proposition that an employer may "subject" an employee to the detriment of harassment when, in circumstances which he can control, he causes or permits the harassment to take place, has been severely limited by the House of Lords judgment in *Advocate General for Scotland v MacDonald*.**

Burton and Rhule v De Vere Hotels 1996
A function room was hired to a third party who booked the comedian Bernard Manning as guest speaker. During Manning's speech, which contained—not surprisingly—an amount of racially and sexually offensive material, he saw the two applicants, waitresses of Afro-Caribbean ethnic origin, and made racially offensive remarks both to them and about them. They complained to the hotel management, their employer, who moved them away from working in that location. They then brought an action against their employer for racial harassment.

Held: (EAT) Finding for the applicants, the EAT stated that "an employer subjects an employee to the detriment of racial harassment if he causes or permits the racial harassment to occur in circumstances in which he can control whether it happens or not." *Per* Smith J. [1996] I.R.L.R. 596.

Commentary
The court was faced with a potentially difficult situation here—Manning was not an employee of the hotel, nor was there any contractual relationship between them, nor perhaps could the hotel be said to have been responsible for Manning's actions. Although the hotel apparently acted reasonably by moving the waitresses, the EAT held that this was not enough; the hotel should have given thought to the risk of the event, and having identified the risk, acted on it to protect its staff. Thus, argued the EAT, under the principle of "good employment practice", the harassment was foreseeable and the hotel did have control over the situation, thus they must accept responsibility. However, the House of Lords in *Advocate General for Scotland v MacDonald* [2003] S.L.T. 1158 disapproved this reasoning, stating that the hotel's failure to give any thought to what may happen to the waitresses was not based on racial grounds, since white waitresses would have been treated in the same way. They also doubted whether the concept of "good employment practice" has any role to play in determining liability in such a case. The case of *Burton v De Vere Hotels* should therefore no longer be relied upon.

Defences

Key Principle: **Apart from the statutory exceptions and defences under the relevant Acts, probably the best way for an employer to escape liability is to have in place and operate a comprehensive and effective equal treatment policy.**

Balgobin and Francis v London Borough of Tower Hamlets 1987
The applicants complained to their employer that they had been harassed by another member of staff. The employer conducted an investigation, during which time the alleged aggressor was suspended, but it was inconclusive. All three members of staff then were required to work together once more. The applicants then brought a claim for sexual harassment against the employer.

Held: (EAT) Two issues were considered. Firstly, the court held that the employer was not liable for harassment by requiring the applicants to work with an alleged harasser. Secondly, the employer's defence would succeed in that it was shown that they had taken all reasonably practical steps to prevent harassment by proper staff supervision and having in place and making known their equal opportunities policy. [1987] I.C.R. 829.

Commentary
It is important to note that the employer should have in place a published complaints procedure and should carry out a full and proper investigation into complaints. Also, it is obviously not sufficient for an employer to have an equal treatment policy; such a policy must be made known to all staff and acted upon when necessary.

Disability Discrimination

Key Principle: **The tribunal should adopt a purposive approach when considering the question of whether a person has a disability for the purpose of the Disability Discrimination Act.**

Vicary v British Telecommunications plc 1999
Mrs Vicary was employed as a clerical officer. She had a disability in her right arm and hand. Light repetitive work, such as typing and vegetable preparation caused her pain, as did more strenuous one-off tasks, such as moving a chair. She brought a complaint of discrimination contrary to the Disability Discrimination Act against her employers. At first instance, the tribunal found as a question of fact that Mrs Vicary was unable to cut up meat or roast potatoes, carry out DIY tasks, file her nails, iron clothes, shake quilts, groom pets, polish furniture, knit, sew or cut with scissors. They held, however, that such activities were not normal day-to-day activities, as it could not be said that they were carried out by most people on a daily basis. Furthermore, they concluded that her disability was not "substantial".

Held: (EAT) The decision of the tribunal that Mrs Vicary was not disabled within the meaning of the Disability Discrimination

Act was perverse and involved errors of law. There was no need
for the tribunal to refer to the guidance set out in s.3 of the
DDA, once they understood that "substantial" means no more
than more than minor or trivial. The list of tasks which Mrs
Vicary was unable to perform were normal day-to-day activities,
since they were tasks which most people perform on a frequent
or fairly regular basis. It is for the tribunal—not for a doctor or
medical expert—to decide what constitutes normal day-to-day
activity, and also whether, in the light of the evidence, an
impairment is "substantial". [1999] I.R.L.R. 680.

Commentary

This case, along with the case of *Goodwin v The Patent Office*
[1999] I.R.L.R. 4, lays down strong guidelines on the meaning of
disability within the DDA 1995.

Key Principle: **It is the duty of the employer (under s.6 of the
DDA 1995) to make such adjustments as are reasonable so as
not to place a disabled employee under a disadvantage.**

Morse v Wiltshire County Council 1998

Mr. Morse, a road worker with Wiltshire Council, suffered a 20
per cent disability which left him with limited movements in his
right hand and leg; he also suffered from blackouts. When he
returned to work he was unable to drive, to operate power
tools, or work on heights or near water when alone. When a
redundancy situation arose, the council took the view that its
retained workforce must be flexible, and that all should be able
to drive. Mr Morse was assessed as part of the redundancy
selection procedure, and along with others he was selected for
redundancy.

Mr Morse brought an action for disability discrimination, which
was dismissed by the employment tribunal on the grounds that
the employers could not have made adjustments to the job or
working conditions to accommodate Mr Morse. He then
appealed to the EAT.

Held: (EAT) In a reserved judgment the appeal was allowed
and remitted to a freshly constituted employment tribunal.
[1998] I.R.L.R. 352.

Commentary

The case is important, not particularly for its facts, but for the procedure laid down by the EAT. An employment tribunal hearing a case of disability discrimination must go through a series of steps, as follows:

(a) The tribunal must decide whether the provisions of ss.6(1) and 6(2) impose a s.6(1) duty on the employer in this particular situation.

(b) If such a duty is imposed, the tribunal must consider whether the employer has taken all such steps as are reasonable in the circumstances.

(c) The tribunal should then consider whether the employer could have taken any of the particular steps laid out in s.6(3).

(d) At the same time the tribunal should consider the reasonableness of taking such steps, as detailed in s.6(4).

(e) If the tribunal finds that the employer has failed to comply with a s.6 duty, it must then decide whether the employer's failure to comply is justified (s.5(2)(b)).

(f) The tribunal must apply an objective test, asking not only whether the employer's reason for the failure was reasonable, but also asking what possible steps the employer could have taken, before reaching its own decision on what steps were reasonable.

Williams v Channel 5 Engineering Services Ltd 1997

Mr Williams, who was profoundly deaf, applied for work as a Channel 5 re-tuner. He attended a three day training course, and successfully completed the first two days, but because of the nature of the finals day's training and the lack of a one-to-one trainer, he was unable to complete the course at that time. Some 10 days later he was provided with the trainer and successfully passed the final examination. However, the delay in training led to a delay in obtaining his identity card. By the time the identity card was received the requirement for re-tuners was diminishing, and Mr Williams was never deployed.

Defending a claim of unlawful discrimination on the grounds of disability, the employer argued that they had no duty to make adjustments, as required under s.6 DDA, until Mr Williams had completed the training course.

Held: (ET) Finding for Mr Williams, the tribunal stated that employers have a duty to plan ahead by considering the needs of future disabled employees. Case 2302136/97.

Commentary
The company should have been aware of Mr Williams' disability and consequent requirements as he was accepted for training, and at that time have made the necessary arrangements and adjustments.

Matty v Tesco Stores Ltd 1997
Mr Matty, a diabetic, applied for a position as a fitter at one of Tesco's distribution centres. The work involved fitters working alone on a shift basis, climbing ladders, and working in refrigerated areas. Tesco consulted with their occupational health advisor and decided that a diabetic employed in such a position would be at risk. They also considered possible adjustments but decided that adjustments were not practicable. Consequently, although Mr Matty was the best candidate, he was not offered the position. Mr Matty then brought a complaint of unlawful discrimination on the grounds of disability.

Held: (ET) There was a risk for a diabetic working under such conditions. Adjustments were not reasonably practicable; racking could not be lowered, refrigerated rooms could not be operated at a higher temperature, altering the hours worked would not have helped, and for reasons of cost it was not possible to employ two fitters on the shift so as to enable Mr Matty to undertake only non-risk work. Case 1901114/97.

Commentary
One of a number of cases defining the s.6 duty of the employer to make such adjustments as are "reasonable".

Key Principle: **It may not be necessary for the employer to be aware of the employee's disability.**

O'Neill v Symm & Co Ltd (1998)
The company dismissed Ms O'Neill for repeated absences from work, not realizing that she was suffering from ME. Ms O'Neill brought an action under the DDA.

Held: (EAT) As the employer was not aware that Ms O'Neill was suffering from a disability under the Act, they could not be liable for unlawful discrimination. [1998] I.R.L.R. 233.

Commentary
Although this appears straightforward and sensible, the later EAT decision in *HJ Heinz Co Ltd v Kenrick* [2000] I.R.L.R. 144 argues that there is nothing in the DDA to require a "subjective" test of discrimination—in other words, there is no requirement that the employer had knowledge of the disability; it is sufficient that the employee had the disability and that the actions of the employer ("objectively" in breach of the Act) were therefore unlawful. A further case, however, *Callaghan v Glasgow City Council* (unreported 2001) prefers the reasoning of *O'Neill*.

Discrimination on the grounds of Religion or Belief

Key Principle: **Following the introduction (into force on December 2, 2003) of the Employment Equality (Religion or Belief) Regulations 2003, it is unlawful to discriminate on the grounds of religion or belief in employment. The regulations cover direct and indirect discrimination, harassment and victimization.**

Case law is not yet available in this area, but the Regulations have considerable impact on issues raised by such cases as *Mandla v Dowell Lee, Seide, et al.*

---

5. OTHER STATUTORY RIGHTS

National Minimum Wage Act 1998

Key Principle: **Although the definition of a "worker" under the Act is much wider than s.230 of the ERA definition of an "employee", the courts have set limits as to its scope.**

Edmonds v Lawson 2000

Ms Edmonds had accepted a 12 month unpaid pupillage with a barristers' chambers. She sought a declaration that the pupillage constituted an apprenticeship, and that she was therefore a "worker" within the meaning of the National Minimum Wage Act 1998, and, being over 26 years of age, she was entitled to be paid the national minimum wage during her pupillage. At first instance she was successful, but a barrister belonging to chambers appealed on the grounds that the pupillage did not constitute a contract since Ms Edmonds had provided no consideration, and furthermore, that the relationship was governed by Bar Council guidelines and that no further contract was necessary.

Held: (CA) Although it was held that a contract between the parties did exist—Ms Edmonds' agreement to a potentially mutually beneficial relationship amounting to consideration—the contract did not constitute an apprenticeship since Ms Edmonds was not "bound" to serve a master. [2000] I.R.L.R. 391.

Commentary

This was friendly litigation brought under the instigation of the Bar Council in order to clarify a point of construction.

Working Time Regulations 1998

Key Principle: **The Working Time Regulations apply to all contracts of employment.**

Barber v RJB Mining UK Ltd 1999

Pit deputies and colliery overmen at a privatised colliery were being required under their contract of employment to work in excess of 48 hours per week. The employer argued that the men were only being asked to work their normal hours and the Working Time Directive, and consequently the Working Time Regulations, was not to be read as forming part of the contract of employment.

Held: (QBD) The Directive, and by implication the Regulations, is a mandatory requirement and applies to all contracts of employment. [1999] I.R.L.R. 308.

Commentary
Unless the employment is specifically excluded by the Regulations, the Regulations are imposed as a term of all employment contracts.

Bowden v Tuffnells Parcels Express Ltd 2001

Mrs Bowden was employed as "batcher", receiving and sorting consignment notes in an office within the employer's road transport business. She worked on a part-time basis and was not contractually entitled to paid holiday. There is provision within Reg.13 of the Working Time Regulations for all employees to be entitled to paid holidays. The employer, however, argued that under Reg.18 the road transport industry was exempt from a number of the Regulations, including Reg.13. The question for the court, therefore, was whether all workers within the excluded sectors of activity were excluded from the regulations, or whether the exclusions applied only to certain types of worker, *e.g.* mobile workers—lorry drivers, etc.

Held: (ECJ) In the opinion of the court, it was the intention of the Council when adopting the Directive to exclude from its scope all workers within particular sectors, including transport. Thus Mrs Bowden and other office workers within the transport industry may have no entitlement to, *e.g.* statutory minimum holiday periods. Case C–133/00.

Commentary
This is an example of the ECJ adopting what appears to be a literal or "black-letter" approach to the law, rather than the purposive approach one might expect. The outcome of this case is obviously unfair—but it should be pointed out that since August 1, 2003 implementation of Directive 2000/34 as national secondary legislation has restricted the exclusion of such workers in industries such as road transport to "mobile workers" only.

Key Principle: **Holiday pay should not be included within an hourly rate of pay unless specifically agreed with the employee.**

Blackburn v (1) Gridquest Ltd (t/a Select Employment) (2) Piper Group plc (3) XR Associates Ltd 2002

The employer had paid what was claimed to be an all inclusive rate of pay, the pay including holiday pay. The tribunal made findings of fact that (a) the employer had not told the employees specifically that the rate of pay included holiday pay, and (b) that the rate of pay did include holiday pay.

Held: (CA) As there was no contractual agreement that holiday pay was included in the rate of pay, the employers were in effect attempting to vary the contract of employment by claiming that it was—their action therefore amounted to either a reduction in wages or an unlawful deduction from wages. [2002] I.R.L.R. 604.

Commentary
This case suggests that there is not necessarily a problem with paying an all inclusive hourly or weekly rate of pay—as long as the contract makes clear that the rate includes holiday pay. However, the Scottish EAT in the case of *MPD Structures Ltd v Munro* [2002] I.R.L.R. 601 stated that holiday pay should not be included with pay, but should be held by the company so as to be available to the employee at the actual time of the holiday; an appeal against this finding has recently been dismissed by the Court of Sessions [2003] S.L.T. 551; consequently, it would appear that holiday pay should be kept separately by the company until the employee actually takes the holiday entitlement, or of course the contract is terminated. In a more recent case on this issue, the EAT in *Marshalls Clay Products Ltd v Caulfield* (July 24, 2003) held that holiday pay may be paid either as a lump sum or as a "rolled-up" amount within the hourly rate as long as the employer had the express agreement of the employee.

Maternity Rights

Key Principle: **Dismissal on pregnancy related grounds may be actionable either as being automatically unfair under s.99(1)(a) of the ERA 1995 or as sex discrimination under SDA 1975.**

Webb v EMO Air Cargo Ltd 1995
Mrs Webb had been hired by EMO Air Cargo, a small company employing 16 people, as a replacement for one of their staff who was absent on maternity leave. It was envisaged that Mrs Webb

would continue to work with EMO once the maternity replacement period was over. Some two weeks after starting work, Mrs Webb discovered that she was pregnant. On learning of this, her employer dismissed her. Mrs Webb brought a claim alleging sex discrimination.

Held: (HL) In confirming a finding for the applicant, the House of Lords made the following points: Discrimination on the grounds of pregnancy is sex discrimination. There is no need for the applicant to compare herself to a "sick man"—pregnancy is a condition, not an illness. [1995] I.R.L.R. 645.

Commentary
Although a similar case today may be brought under s.99 of the ERA—dismissal on the grounds of pregnancy being automatically unfair—a sex discrimination claim may be advantageous because it would also cover the recruitment process, and, unlike unfair dismissal claims, there is no upper limit on the amount of compensation which may be awarded.

It is possible that the dismissal may have been held to be fair had Mrs Webb been appointed *only* on a fixed term contract, but see the case of *Carunana v Manchester Airport plc* [1996] I.R.L.R. 378 which appears to clarify this point.

Rees v Apollo Watch Repairs plc 1996
When Ms Rees left to take maternity leave, her employer engaged a replacement. The replacement was found to be more efficient than Ms Rees, and Ms Rees was consequently dismissed. The tribunal, sitting before the judgment in *Webb*, held that the dismissal was on the grounds of Ms Rees' efficiency, not on the grounds of her pregnancy.

Held: (EAT) The Employment Appeal Tribunal found that the underlying reason for the dismissal was Ms Rees' pregnancy and maternity leave. Had she not taken maternity leave, no replacement would have been engaged and no dismissal would have resulted. [1996] I.C.R. 466.

Commentary
The court will apply maternity related legislation purposively, and it may not be possible for an employer to avoid liability by seeking to adopt a purely literal approach to the issue.

Key Principle: **Protection afforded to pregnant workers may not extend to pregnancy related illnesses.**

Handels-og Kontorfunkionaerernes Forbund i Danmark (for Larsson) v Dansk Handel & Service (for Foxted Supermaked A/S) 1997
Ms Larsson advised her employer in August 1991 that she was pregnant. During her pregnancy she took sick leave for two weeks in August and again from November until her statutory maternity leave period began in March 1992. At the end of her maternity leave she took annual holiday until October, but did not return to work due to illness. Her estimated date for return to work was given as January 1993. In November 1992 her employer dismissed her by letter due to her lengthy absence and the fact that she was unable to return to work in the near future. Ms Larsson claimed that her dismissal was contrary to Directive 76/207, since her illness had begun during her pregnancy and had continued through and after her maternity leave period.

Held: (ECJ) The Pregnant Workers Directive 92/85 makes it clear that absence during the protected period, unless unconnected with the worker's condition, could not be considered as grounds for a dismissal; however, the court in the case of *Aldi* (C–179/88 [1991] I.R.L.R. 31, had found that an illness manifesting itself after maternity leave had ended should be treated in the same way as any other illness, and may therefore give grounds for a potentially fair dismissal. The court found that it therefore followed that Directive 76/207, the Equal Treatment Directive, did not preclude dismissal for absence, even if that absence was due to a pregnancy related cause, if the absence extended beyond the period of maternity leave. [1997] I.R.L.R. 643.

Commentary
The court thus considered the question of whether a pregnancy related illness should be treated as an illness or as part of the pregnancy. Two further cases should be considered, as follows.

Caledonia Bureau Investment & Property Ltd v Caffrey 1998
Ms Caffrey, prior to the expiry of her maternity leave, submitted a series of medical certificates to the effect that she could not resume work until the end of November 1996 due to post-natal

depression. On November 28 her employer dismissed her with four weeks' pay in lieu of notice.

Held: (EAT) supported the findings of the tribunal that Ms Caffrey had been unfairly dismissed for a reason connected with pregnancy or childbirth. They stated that under s.99 of the ERA 1995 if a pregnancy related illness arose during the period of maternity leave and extended beyond the maternity leave, a dismissal arising from that illness would be discriminatory, on condition that the contract of employment had been specifically extended beyond the period of maternity leave. [1998] I.C.R. 603.

Commentary
In this case it should be remembered that the employer had accepted medical certificates from Ms Caffrey prior to her dismissal, thus extending her contract beyond the expiry of her maternity leave.

Brown v Rentokil Ltd 1998
There was a term in employment contracts with Rentokil that employees absent for more than 26 continuous weeks would be dismissed. Mrs Brown was unable to work due to pregnancy related illnesses, and at the end of a 26 week period she was dismissed.

Held: (ECJ) Declining to follow the earlier case of *Larsson*, the court held that the dismissal of an employee for pregnancy related illness during pregnancy amounted to direct sex discrimination. Further, the position of a pregnant worker unable to work due to pregnancy related illness could not be compared with that of a man unable to work for a similar period of time due to illness. [1998] I.R.L.R. 445.

Commentary
Despite the cases of *Brown* and *Caledonia Bureau*, it appears that minimal protection is given to female workers who are dismissed due to pregnancy related illness, if that illness does not manifest itself before the expiry of the maternity leave period.

6. HEALTH AND SAFETY

Common Law

Key Principle: **At common law, the employer owes a duty of care to his employees as individuals.**

Paris v Stepney Borough Council 1951
Mr Paris worked as a cleaner, part of his duties consisted of scraping rust from the underside of vehicles. It was not normal practice for the employer to provide goggles for this task. Mr Paris had only one good eye, and when a splinter of rust entered this eye, Mr Paris was totally blinded.

Held: (HL) The employer owes a duty of care not only to employees generally, but to each employee as an individual. Thus in the case of Mr Paris the employer should have foreseen there was a risk of greater injury and acted accordingly. [1951] 1 All E.R. 42.

Commentary
Consequently, if a particular employee may be particularly susceptible to a danger, the employer would have a duty to take particular care. One of the main reasons for the rise in pictorial, rather than purely written, warning signs in factories, etc. is that employers are aware that some employees may be illiterate or have difficulty reading English, and the employer recognises that they have a duty to warn *all* employees.

Key Principle: **The duty of care is owed by the employer and may not be delegated—although the performance of the duty may be.**

Wilsons and Clyde Coal Co Ltd v English 1938
Mr English was employed in mine-working when he was injured by machinery. The employer maintained that they had employed a colliery agent, as they were required to do by law, and since part of the agent's role was safety of the mine, the agent rather than the employer was liable.

Held: (HL) The responsibility for the health and safety of employees must lie with the employer. [1938] A.C. 57.

Commentary
Thus, although performance of health and safety duties may be delegated, the responsibility remains with the employer.

Key Principle: **The employer's duty extends to providing safe plant and equipment, a safe place of work, a safe system of work, and competent fellow employees.**

Bradford v Robinson Rentals 1967
In a spell of particularly cold weather, the employee was required to make a round trip of some 400 miles in a company van that had no heater and cracked windows. The employee suffered frostbite and brought an action against his employer.

Held: (QB) The employer was liable for failing to supply suitable plant. [1967] 1 All E.R. 267.

Commentary
The case is authority for both "safe plant" and "safe place of work", since it was held by the court that a van could constitute a place of work.

Taylor v Rover Car Co Ltd 1966
The company bought a batch of chisels from a reputable supplier, unfortunately due to a manufacturing defect, the chisels had been improperly hardened and thus prone to splinter when used. When in use at Rover one chisel did splinter without causing damage, later a second chisel also shattered causing injury to an employee's eye.

Held: (CA) The employer was liable. Following the failure of the first chisel, the employer was aware of the potential danger from that batch of tools, but failed to act on this knowledge. [1966] 2 All E.R. 181.

Commentary
Once the employer becomes aware of a danger they have a duty to take action to protect their employees.

Berry v Stone Manganese Co Ltd 1972
The employee worked in an area of the works in which noise level was high. The employer provided ear defenders but little effort was made to ensure that employees actually wore them.

Held: (QB) In view of the known danger to employees from the high noise level, and in view of the fact that the danger may not have been apparent to many of the employees, the employer had a duty to ensure that protective equipment was not only supplied, but also actually used. [1972] 1 Lloyds Rep. 182.

Commentary
This case addresses problems faced by many employers. Often employees will be reluctant to make proper use of safety equipment—it may restrict their movement, it may be hot or uncomfortable, etc. In such situations, especially if the risk of injury is known by the employer, but not apparent to the employee, the employer must take steps to impress upon the employees the need for the equipment, to the extent of dismissing employees who refuse to comply.

Hudson v Ridge Manufacturing Co Ltd 1957
Over a period of some four years, and despite repeated warnings from the foreman, an employee had played "practical jokes" on other employees, including deliberately tripping them. On the final occasion, a fellow employee was tripped and was injured.

Held: (QB) The company were aware of the behaviour of the practical joker and should have taken steps to prevent it. Thus, the company could not escape liability. [1957] 2 Q.B. 348.

Commentary
The presence of the practical joker constituted a danger to fellow employees, the company by not stopping the danger were in effect accepting it, and consequently accepting the liability.

Latimer v AEC Ltd 1953
Following a heavy storm, the floor of the employer's factory became flooded. The water mixed with oils used in the manufacturing process and left the floor in a dangerously slippery state. Sawdust was laid over most of the floor, but there was insufficient to cover the entire floor area. An employee slipped on part of the untreated floor and was injured.

Held: (HL) The employer was held not to be liable. Reasonable precautions had been taken, and the court held that the danger was not sufficient to warrant closing the entire factory down. [1953] A.C. 643.

Commentary
The duty of the employer is not absolute; it is the duty to act as a *reasonable* employer would act in those circumstances.

Johnstone v Bloomsbury HA 1991
The case concerned an action brought by a junior hospital doctor against his employers seeking a declaration that it was unlawful for them to require him to work longer than 72 hours per week, despite provision in the contract of employment that he may be called upon to work up to 88 hours per week.

Held: (CA) In a majority decision the Court of Appeal held in favour of the junior doctor. The reason for the decision was either that requiring overtime hours to be worked was merely an optional right on the part of the employer which must be exercised with regard to the employee's health (Browne-Wilkinson V-C), or that even if the contract allowed it, the right to require an employee to work up to 88 hours per week must be exercised subject to other contractual terms, particularly the term regarding health and safety. [1991] I.C.R. 269.

Commentary
The case also gives rise to the question of whether the Unfair Contract Terms Act 1977 applies to contracts of employment, a question that was later answered in the affirmative in *Brigden v American Express Bank Ltd* [2000] I.R.L.R. 94, Q.B.D.

Walker v Northumberland County Council 1995
Mr Walker worked for the social services department of the county council, as a senior social services manager. Over the years the workload within the department had increased considerably, including a large number of child abuse cases. Despite a number of requests from Mr Walker, no additional staff were provided to help cope with the workload. Mr Walker suffered a nervous breakdown, but shortly resumed work in his old position. Extra staff were provided, but after a short period were withdrawn. Within a few months Mr Walker had again suffered a nervous breakdown, and was dismissed by his employers on the grounds of permanent ill health.

Held: (QBD) The first issue for the court was to decide whether the duty of care owed by the employer for the safety of the employee extended beyond physical injury to the areas of psychiatric damage. The court found there was no logical reason why it should not. The court then held that the second nervous breakdown had been foreseeable, and that the employer's failure to provide support amounted to a failure to fulfill their duty to provide a safe system of work. [1995] I.R.L.R. 35.

Commentary
This decision should not be taken as giving *carte blanche* to work stress related claims as such; the court only considered Mr Walker's second nervous breakdown, for which, it is argued, there were clear warning signs.

Sutherland v Hatton; Somerset County Council v Barber; Sandwell Metropolitan Borough Council v Jones; Baker Refractories Ltd v Bishop 2002
Four joined cases were heard by the Court of Appeal, all the cases concerned appeals against awards for psychiatric illness or injury caused to the employee by stress at work.

Held: (CA) The court laid down a number of important points for consideration in cases of stress related illness or injury at work:

(a) The ordinary principles of employers' liability apply to claims for stress related illness or injury.

(b) It must be decided whether this kind of injury to this particular employer was reasonably foreseeable.

(c) Foreseeability depends upon what the employer knows or ought to know.

(d) The test should be the same for all occupations; no occupations should be considered intrinsically more dangerous to mental health than others.

(e) The employer should consider both the nature and extent of the work done by the employee, and any signs or indications from the employee of impending problems or vulnerability.

(f) Generally, the employer is entitled to take what he is told by the employee at face value.

(g) In deciding to act and in deciding the steps to be taken, the employer should act as a reasonable employer of a similar size and with similar resources would act.

(h) The employer can only reasonably be expected to take action which is likely to do some good.

(i) An employer operating a confidential advice and referral service to those employees identified as being at risk is unlikely to be found in breach of duty of care.

(j) If the only reasonable course of action available to an employer would be demotion or dismissal of the employee, an employer who allows a willing employee to continue in their existing role will not normally be in breach of their duty.

(k) The employer should, in any case, only be liable for the damage caused by their own wrongdoing; if the illness or injury is caused by multiple factors the issue of apportionment arises. [2002] P.I.Q.R. 21.

Commentary
This is a useful case to read in full. Between them, the four case studies cover many of the problems encountered in this area of law, and the court's judgment indicates the approach to be taken in future cases.

Defences

Key principle: **Whereas the partial defence of contributory negligence may be commonly proven, the complete defence of *volenti non fit injuria* is rarely successful.**

ICI Ltd v Shatwell 1965
Two shotfirers deliberately broke both statutory regulations and the employer's instructions, resulting in injury to both of them. One of them then brought an action against the employer on the basis of their vicarious liability for the actions of the other shotfirer.

Held: (HL) The employer was not liable. The complete defence of *volenti non fit injuria* succeeded. [1965] A.C. 656.

Commentary
The idea that an employee freely consents to the risk of danger and injury is obviously, in most cases, false. In most contracts of employment the employer has the stronger position, consequently even apparent agreement by the employee to the risk of danger can hardly be said to be freely given.

Key Principle: **The employer will be vicariously liable for the actions of his employees carried out "in the course of employment". However, this phrase has been interpreted more restrictively than in discrimination cases.**

Kay v ITW Ltd 1968
A fork lift truck driver found that his way was blocked by a lorry. Although he had no specific instruction to do so, he moved the lorry himself, and in so doing injured another employee.

Held: (CA) The employer was held to be vicariously liable, since the action was not so extreme as to take it outside of his normal activities. [1968] 1 Q.B. 140.

Commentary
The question here is one of where the line should be drawn. Each case is considered on its own facts. In the above case, the employer would reasonably argue that it is no part of a fork lift driver's job to drive lorries—but the job specification or practice of most employees is not sufficiently specific to allow that argument to be relied upon in many cases.

Hilton v Thomas Burton Ltd 1961
An employee made use of the firm's van to drive to a café on an unauthorised work break. In so doing he knocked down and killed a fellow worker.

Held: (Assizes) Although the employee had the general permission of the employer to drive the van, at the time of the incident he was acting outside the course of his employment. Thus the employer was not liable. [1961] 1 W.L.R. 705.

Commentary
In this case, the employee is carrying out an action—the driving of the van—which is part of his overall job, but the manner and the

time at which he is carrying it out takes it outside of his "course of employment".

Is it therefore relevant for whose benefit the action is being performed? Had the employee been taking the van on an unauthorised trip to pick up a spare part for a machine, would the decision have been the same?

Lister v Hesley Hall Ltd 2001
The employer was a boys' boarding school, one of whose employees committed acts of gross indecency against a number of the boarders. The question for the court was in regard to the employer's liability at common law for the actions of its employee.

Held: (HL) The correct approach was to ask whether the actions of the employee were so closely connected with his employment to find the employer vicariously liable. In this case, the employee's position as warden and the close contact with the pupils that the position required satisfied the test; the employer should therefore be found liable. [2001] I.R.L.R. 472.

Commentary
An important judgment which moves away from the narrower common law test of the past. It is at present a little unclear how widely the courts will construe this approach (*cf. Jones v Tower Boot*), but the House of Lords in the recent case of *Dubai Aluminium v Salachi* were content to apply *Lister*.

Statutory Provisions

Key Principle: **Many of the statutory duties of an employer are not absolute. They require that the employer should take "reasonable" steps.**

West Bromwich Building Society v Townsend 1983
An HSE inspector alleged that the employer had not taken sufficient steps to ensure the protection of its employees by failing to erect bandit screens on its counters.

Held: (QBD) Since the danger of attack was relatively slight, the staff had all been trained not to resist attack, and the screens would appear contrary to the society's customer-friendly image, the court held that the society had done everything reasonably practicable. [1983] I.C.R. 257.

Commentary
This is an early case brought under this legislation, and it appears that the court adopted the attitude that it was for the employer to decide the best method of dealing with perceived risks.

R v Gateway Foodsmarkets Ltd 1997
Despite regular maintenance by a reputable company, a lift in one of the company's stores often gave trouble and jammed. The lift could be freed by manually tripping an electrical contact in the lift motor room, the store staff had been told how to do this by the lift contractors, and it was the practice for one of the staff to enter the lift room and free the switch, rather than to call out the lift contractors. The company head office was not aware of this practice. On one occasion one of the store managers entered the lift room in order to free the lift, and fell through a trap door which had been left open, resulting in his death.

Held: (CA) The company must accept liability. A failure by the company at either head office or store level to take reasonable precautions to protect the health and safety of its employees must amount to a breach of duty under the Health and Safety at Work Act 1974. [1997] I.R.L.R. 189.

Commentary
Thus the company was found liable, despite the fact that the head office were not aware of the practice undertaken at store level.

The Court of Appeal also doubted whether properly this was a case of vicarious liability; stating that since a company could only act through its servants or agents, the liability may be regarded as the company's own.

Cullen v North Lanarkshire Council 1998
Whilst unloading materials from a lorry and throwing them into a skip, Mr Cullen tripped on some of the materials and fell from the lorry injuring himself. He brought an action under the Manual Handling Operations Regulations, but the court at first instance held that the Regulations applied only to risk of injury through lifting and not through tripping.

Held: (CS) The Regulations should apply to all aspects of manual handling, and not merely to lifting. [1998] S.C. 451.

Commentary
The Court refused to accept the literal interpretation of the
Regulations as supported by the employer, and instead adopted a
purposive approach.

Stark v The Post Office 2000
Mr Stark was employed by the Post Office as a postman, and he
was supplied with a bicycle for his delivery rounds. One day
whilst working, part of the front brake broke and lodged in the
wheel, causing Mr Stark to be thrown to the ground and suffer
injury. It was accepted that a prior inspection of the brake
would not have revealed the defect. Mr Stark, however, maintained that Reg.6 of the Provision and Use of Work Equipment
Regulations 1992 imposed an absolute obligation on the
employer that work equipment was maintained in an efficient
state, in efficient working order and in good repair.

Held: (CA) Although the Directives (Work Equipment Directive 89/655 and Framework Directive 89/391) *may* lay down a
less than absolute duty, the same was not true of the Regulations. The Directives should be taken as laying down minimum standards, whereas the Regulations are so drafted as to
impose an absolute obligation. [2000] I.C.R. 1013.

Commentary
Thus Reg.6(1) lays down an obligation on employers to ensure
that work equipment is maintained in an efficient state, in efficient
working order and in good repair; and it is no defence that the
defect may not have been identified in the course of even a
thorough inspection.

---

7. TERMINATION OF EMPLOYMENT

Key Principle: **It is possible that the contract of employment
may be terminated, without giving rise to a dismissal.**

Egg Stores (Stamford Hill) Ltd v Leibovici 1977
Mr Leibovici had been employed by Egg Stores for some 15
years. He suffered injury in a road accident and was absent

from work for almost six months. For the first two months of his absence he was paid sick pay by the company. When he was able to return to work, the company advised him that he was no longer required, as a suitable replacement had been engaged. He claimed unfair dismissal, and the company responded that the contract of employment had been frustrated.

Held: (EAT) The court laid down a number of factors which should be taken into account when considering whether an employment contract has been frustrated:

(a) the length of the previous employment;

(b) how long it had been expected that the employment would continue;

(c) the nature of the job;

(d) the nature, length and effect of the illness or disabling event;

(e) the need of the employer for the work to be done, and the need for a replacement to do it;

(f) the risk to the employer of acquiring obligations in respect of redundancy payments or compensation for unfair dismissal to the replacement employee;

(g) whether wages have continued to be paid;

(h) the acts and statements of the employer in relation to the employment, including the dismissal of, or failure to dismiss, the employee; and

(i) whether in all the circumstances a reasonable employer could be expected to wait any longer. [1977] I.C.R. 260.

Commentary

Frustration may be defined as an extraneous event, unforeseen by the parties—and therefore unplanned for in the contract—which is the fault of neither party and has the effect of making the contract either impossible to perform, or would make performance substantially different from that agreed. It may therefore be thought that to hold that frustration does not give rise to a dismissal is somewhat harsh on the employee, but convenient for the employer.

Shepherd & Co Ltd v Jerrom 1986

Mr Jerrom was almost one year into a four year apprenticeship when he was sentenced to a six month custodial sentence. On his release, his employer claimed that the contract had been frustrated and no longer operated.

Held: (CA) The court confirmed the reasoning of Lord Denning M.R. in the earlier case of *Hare v Murphy Brothers* [1974] I.R.L.R. 342, and held that a term of imprisonment is capable of frustrating the contract of employment. [1986] I.R.L.R. 358.

Commentary

Since frustration of the contract must be brought about by an event which is the fault of neither party, the argument had been raised that the commission of a crime which led to the imprisonment must be viewed as the fault of the employee—and could not therefore amount to frustration. Lord Denning had argued that commission of the crime was not the frustrating event; the frustrating event was the imposition by the court of a term of imprisonment—had the court awarded a suspended sentence or a fine, there would have been no grounds for frustration of the contract. Furthermore, it was established that long-term illness may give rise to frustration, to the detriment of the employee, consequently it was inequitable that an employee, absent from work for perhaps a similar period of time due to the commission of a crime, should be treated more favourably.

8. WRONGFUL DISMISSAL

Key Principle: **Dismissal without notice may, on occasion, be quite lawful.**

Pepper v Webb 1969

The plaintiff was a gardener, about whom there had been a number of complaints about his inefficiency and insolent manner. On the morning in question the employer's wife asked him to plant certain flowers, he responded: "I am leaving at 12 o'clock; you can do what you like about them. If you don't like it you can give me notice." The employer then went to remonstrate with the gardener, asking why he was making such a fuss over a half-hour job. The gardener replied: "I couldn't care less about your bloody greenhouse and your sodding garden." He then walked off. The employer gave him immediate notice of termination of his contract. The gardener then sued for monies in lieu of notice.

Held: (CA) The instruction from the employer's wife was reasonable and lawful; the gardener's wilful disobedience of the instruction amounted to a repudiation of his contract. Therefore, the employer was justified in dismissing the employee summarily. [1969] 1 W.L.R. 514.

Commentary
Obviously, instances of gross misconduct may allow the employer to lawfully dismiss without notice. However, in deciding what constitutes gross misconduct, the court will look not only to the words or actions, but also to their factual background.

Wilson v Racher 1974
Mr Wilson was head gardener to Mr Racher. It appears that Mr Racher either set extremely, if not impossibly, high standards within his gardens, or that he was determined to "get rid of" Mr Wilson. On the relevant day an argument developed, apparently instigated by Mr Racher, in the course of which Mr Racher accused his gardener of several alleged infringements, and of shirking his work. At one point Mr Wilson was provoked into saying: "If you remember it was pissing with rain on Friday. Do you expect me to get fucking wet?" After further argument Mr Wilson was summarily dismissed, and sought to recover monies in lieu of notice.

Held: (CA) The court found, that unlike the case of *Pepper v Webb*, this was not a case of wilful disobedience. Although the employee has a duty of obedience, along with a duty of courtesy and respect towards his employer, there were in this case special circumstances amounting to goading and provoking of the employee. Consequently, Mr Wilson's action should succeed. [1974] I.C.R. 428.

Commentary
By looking beyond the actual words to the background of the situation the court distinguished the earlier case of *Pepper v Webb*.

Key Principle: **It is not completely settled law what effect the repudiatory breach may have on the contract.**

Thomas Marshall (Exports) Ltd v Guinle 1979

Guinle was appointed as managing director of Thomas Marshall on a 10 year contract. The contract contained various exclusions, including restrictions on the use of the company's confidential information. Guinle, however, broke those terms and used company information for his own purposes whilst still employed under the contract. He then argued that since he had committed a fundamental breach of the contract, he could no longer be held to its terms. In other words, he argued that his fundamental breach of contract had determined the contract without the need for the company to accept the breach.

Held: (Ch.D) The court rejected the argument put before it that the contract of employment was unlike the general rule of contract and may be determined by a fundamental breach by one party—even if that breach was *intended* to bring the contract to an end. The reasoning was based partly on the line of authority dating back to the case of *Lumley v Wagner* (1852) in which the court had issued an injunction restraining a singer from appearing elsewhere whilst still under an original contract. Furthermore, it appeared unjust that the innocent party should be denied the right to elect how to treat the breach. [1979] Ch 227.

Commentary

This is an example of the "bilateral" or "elective" theory. It explains how an employer may obtain an injunction to restrain an employee through a term in the contract, even though the contract in other respects may have been brought to an effective end by a repudiatory breach.

Rigby v Ferodo Ltd 1988

The company imposed a 5 per cent wage reduction on Mr Rigby and others, even though no actual agreement had been reached between the company, the employees or the trade union. Mr Rigby continued to work normally, and some two years later sued for the return of the lost money.

Held: (HL) "For my part, I can see no reason in law or logic why ... a contract of employment should be on any different footing from any other contract as regards the principle that 'an unaccepted repudiation is a thing writ in water and of no value to anybody'." *Per* Lord Oliver.

Thus the unilateral reduction in wages, amounting to a repudiation by the company, should not take effect until accepted by the employee. [1988] I.C.R. 29.

Commentary

The court did however appreciate that a repudiation in the form of a wrongful dismissal would have the effect of putting an end to the status of employer/employee relationship, but stated that there was no reason why the contract should not remain enforceable in so far as those obligations which do not necessarily depend upon the master—servant relationship.

Although this "elective" or "bilateral" theory probably accurately reflects the law in this area, some concern or doubt has been expressed *obiter* by the Court of Appeal in the case of *Boyo v London Borough of Lambeth* [1995] I.R.L.R. 50.

Key Principle: **Compensation for wrongful dismissal will normally amount only to monies to which the employee would have been contractually entitled had the contract been lawfully terminated, in effect, monies in lieu of notice.**

Addis v Gramaphone Co Ltd 1909

Mr Addis worked as a manager for the company. He was paid a mixture of salary and commission, and his contract made provision for termination on six months' notice. The company gave Mr Addis six months' notice of termination, but then refused to allow him to work the notice period. The case was referred to the House of Lords to determine the level of damages to which Mr Addis was entitled.

Held: (HL) He should be entitled to monies representing his salary for the six month notice period, and to monies representing the commission he would have earned during such a period. He would not, however, be entitled to monies to compensate for injury to feelings, or for any loss he might sustain from the fact that having been dismissed might make it more difficult for him to obtain further employment. [1909] A.C. 488.

Commentary
Thus, unlike a claim for unfair dismissal, a finding of wrongful dismissal will entitle the employee to only those monies to which he is entitled under the contract. However, if in a fixed term contract no notice period is stated, early termination of that contract may enable the employee to claim all monies outstanding under the contract. He would not, however, be entitled to any *discretionary* bonus payments or *discretionary* salary increases.

Malik v Bank of Credit and Commerce International 1997
Mr Malik was dismissed for redundancy when his employer, BCCI, went into liquidation. Mr Malik had worked for the bank for some 12 years, but because of the adverse publicity surrounding the collapse of the bank had found it very difficult to obtain suitable alternative employment. He sought to bring a claim for damages based on a breach of the contract of employment by his employer, namely a breach of the term of mutual trust and confidence caused by the manner in which the bank had managed its affairs.

Held: (HL) It was held that the bank had operated in a corrupt and dishonest manner, and that Mr Malik was innocent of any involvement in such dealings. Such action by the employer had breached the term of mutual trust and confidence.

In considering whether to allow a claim for damages in this action for wrongful dismissal to go ahead, the House of Lords found itself potentially restricted by its earlier decision in *Addis*. The House argued that *Addis* was decided before the term of "mutual trust and confidence" had been recognised, and, further, that the facts concerning the closure of BCCI were unusually extreme; consequently, the applicant's claim may proceed. [1997] I.R.L.R. 462.

Commentary
On the one hand, if a claim for damages for wrongful dismissal is restricted to contractual entitlement only, it is very arguable that it should include compensation for breach of contractual terms; the only problem for the courts being to satisfactorily quantify such damages. On the other hand, despite *dicta* from the House of Lords to the contrary, it was felt likely that the approach in *Malik* may have the effect of opening the floodgates to further wrongful dismissal claims, allowing actions to be brought by those who do not qualify for unfair dismissal to seek compensation for more than merely the notice period.

Johnson v Unisys Ltd 2001
Mr Johnson worked for Unisys from 1971 until 1994, at which time he was summarily dismissed for an alleged breach of contract. He complained to an Employment Tribunal of unfair dismissal, his complaint was upheld and compensation awarded to the sum of £11,700, being the maximum amount at the time, less 25 per cent for his contributory fault. He then brought proceedings in the County Court claiming damages for the manner of his dismissal which had resulted in him suffering a mental breakdown, making it impossible for him to find alternative employment. His claim was dismissed, as was his appeal to the Court of Appeal, who held themselves bound by the principle in *Addis*, that damages for wrongful dismissal did not include compensation for either the manner of, or the effect of, the dismissal. Mr Johnson appealed to the House of Lords.

Held: (HL) In a complex and at times confusing judgment, the House of Lords dismissed Mr Johnson's appeal. Several issues were raised by their Lordships:

(a) Since Mr Johnson's contract with his employer contained a clause permitting them to make a payment in lieu of notice to Mr Johnson, there was no breach of contract as long as the payment made amounted to the wages Mr Johnson would have received had the full notice period been given.

(b) Lord Steyn (dissenting on this point) doubted whether the *ratio* of *Addis* did in fact preclude an award of damages in a case such as *Johnson*, as long as a causal link could be proven.

(c) Since parliament had laid down both a procedure for and a maximum level of compensation for claims in respect of the manner of a dismissal (by way of Unfair Dismissal legislation) it was not for the courts to extend this (note that Mr Johnson was seeking compensation in excess of £400,000). [2001] I.R.L.R. 279.

Commentary
This has become a difficult area of law to understand, particularly in the light of subsequent cases. In the case of *Gogay v Hertfordshire County Council* [2000] I.R.L.R. 703, an award of damages was upheld by the Court of Appeal for a breach of mutual trust and confidence leading to psychiatric injury. In that case the

employee had been suspended from work; had he been dismissed, rather than suspended, it is arguable that following *Johnson* his claim would have been unsuccessful. Further, in the case of *King v University Court of the University of St Andrews* [2002] I.R.L.R. 252, the Court of Sessions distinguished between a breach of mutual trust and confidence during the existence of the contract (for which damages at common law may be claimed) and a breach once the decision to dismiss has been taken by the employer (for which, following *Johnson*, damages at common law would not be available). On this issue, see also the case of *McCabe v Cornwall County Council* [2003] I.R.L.R. 87 in which the Court of Appeal took a similar view to the one expressed in *King*.

Key Principle: **Money in lieu of notice is normally regarded as damages for the breach of contract, and as such will neither be taxable nor liable to the duty to mitigate.**

EMI Group Electronics Ltd v Coldicott (Inspector of Taxes) 1999
Monies paid to two senior managers dismissed on grounds of redundancy included an amount for "pay in lieu of notice", and as such were considered to be non-taxable. Contained in the contracts of employment of the employees was a clause stating: "The company reserves the right to make payment of the equivalent of salary in lieu of notice..." The Revenue determined that such payments were emoluments arising from the employment relationship and therefore taxable.

Held: (CA) A payment in lieu of notice which is made due to a pre-agreed term of the employment contract is to be treated differently to a payment in lieu of notice which is made by way of compensation or damages for breach of the contract. If a payment is made as a result of a contractual term it becomes a payment made "in return for acting as or being an employee" (*per* Lord Radcliffe in *Hochstasser v Mayes* [1960] A.C. 376, HL), and therefore liable to income tax. [1999] I.R.L.R. 630.

Commentary
In many companies in many industries, it is accepted that employees will not be required to work a notice period, but will be paid money in lieu of notice which is not taxable. This will not be

the case in the situation where the employment contact contains a term allowing the employer to pay money in lieu of notice—in such a situation the payment will be liable to income tax.

Cerberus Software Ltd v Rowley 1999

Mr Rowley was employed under a contract of employment which provided for six months' notice of termination to be given by either party, and also provided that the employer could make a payment of monies in lieu of the notice period. Mr Rowley was subsequently dismissed without either notice or money in lieu of notice. After a period of some five weeks he obtained new employment at a higher rate of pay. He brought an action against his previous employer claiming damages for wrongful dismissal. The tribunal awarded Mr Rowley a sum equivalent to six months' pay. Cerberus appealed arguing that if they terminated Mr Rowley's contract without notice or payment of monies in lieu of notice that would indeed amount to wrongful dismissal, but in the awarding of damages for the breach of contract the court should take into account Mr Rowley's duty to mitigate his loss, which amounted to the money he received from his new employment.

Held: (EAT) Monies in lieu of notice may either be claimed as monies due under the contract (see *EMI v Coldicott*), or as damages for the breach of contract which have the effect of putting the employee in the position he would have been in had the breach not occurred. In neither situation was the employer entitled to the benefit of the employee's mitigation, since the employer had agreed in the contract to pay the whole sum, and the breach was the non-payment of that amount. [1999] I.R.L.R. 690.

Commentary

To have held otherwise would have allowed the employer to benefit financially from their breach which would have been inequitable.

9. UNFAIR DISMISSAL

The applicant's ability to claim

Key Principle: Continuity of employment—necessary in order to apply for unfair dismissal in most cases—*may* be preserved though periods when the contract is not actually in force.

Ford v Warwickshire County Council 1983
Mrs Ford was employed by the local authority as a lecturer on a series of contracts, each running from September to July. For the purpose of a redundancy claim, the court was called upon to decide whether continuity of employment was preserved during the summer months when no contract of employment existed.

Held: (HL) The House of Lords held that the period between contracts amounted to a "temporary cessation of work" under s.212(3)(b), and consequently continuity of employment was preserved. [1983] I.R.L.R. 126.

Commentary
Their Lordships adopted a mathematical approach by comparing the period of the break with the periods of work on either side of it. Therefore, as long as the period of the break is sufficiently short in comparison with the length of the work periods, the break may be classified as "temporary cessation".

Flack v Kodak Ltd 1986
Mrs Flack worked at Kodak on a seasonal basis, being laid-off and taken back on, on a number of occasions over a period of some years, as seasonal demand for photographic reproductions fluctuated. At her final dismissal she claimed a redundancy payment. The tribunal applied the mathematical approach from *Ford* and held that, since the periods of work and breaks had been irregular, continuity of employment had not been preserved.

Held: (CA) The court held that where periods of work and break were irregular the approach in *Ford*, of looking at only one cycle of work and break, could lead to a wrong result. The preferable approach with an irregular pattern of breaks and work was to look at several cycles as a whole to determine whether the breaks constituted only temporary cessations. [1986] I.C.R. 775.

Commentary
Thus, if the breaks are regular, the approach in *Ford*, of looking at only the final cycle, would be appropriate; whereas if the breaks are irregular, the approach from *Flack* would be preferred.

Booth v United States of America 1999
Mr Booth worked as a maintenance technician for the United States Army at its base in Southampton. He had been employed under a series of fixed term contracts, each for less than two years, with breaks between the contracts of not less than two weeks. At the termination of the final contract Mr Booth claimed for either redundancy or unfair dismissal (at the time there was a two-year qualifying period for unfair dismissal).

Held: (EAT) Since it was clear from the arrangement that the employer did not wish to treat the employment as continuing over the periods of the breaks, the Employment Tribunal were entitled to find that continuity of employment was not preserved during the break periods, and consequently Mr Booth's claim should fail.

> "If, by so arranging their affairs, employers lawfully are able to employ people in such a manner that the employees cannot complain of unfair dismissal or seek a redundancy payment, that is a matter for them. It is for the legislators, not the courts, to close any loopholes that might be perceived to exist."—*per* Morison J. [1999] I.R.L.R. 16.

Commentary
The court appears to have placed considerable importance on the intentions of the parties—or at least the intentions of the employer, in reaching their conclusions. Certainly the Employment Appeal Tribunal interpreted s.212(3) rather more literally, and less purposively, than did the House of Lords in *Ford*, or the Court of Appeal in *Flack,* neither of which was, perhaps surprisingly, referred to in *Booth*.

Key Principle: **The effective date of termination (EDT) is generally the actual date on which the termination of employment takes effect.**

Dedman v British Building and Engineering Appliances Ltd 1974

The employee was dismissed with immediate effect on May 5, 1972, receiving salary for the month of May, plus one month in lieu of notice. At the time, a claim for unfair dismissal had to be presented within a four-week period. The employee was unaware of this, and apparently his solicitors did not tell him; consequently, he presented his claim for unfair dismissal on June 23. If the EDT was May 5, his application was out of time. Would the court therefore accept the argument that, since he had been paid monies in lieu of notice, the EDT was either May 31, or even the end of June? At first instance, the tribunal had accepted the date of May 31 as the EDT; however this had been rejected on appeal to the Industrial Court. The employee appealed to the Court of Appeal.

Held: (CA) The court ruled that the effect of the employer's letter of May 5 was to terminate the employment with immediate effect on that date. Thus the EDT was May 5, and the employee's claim on June 23, for unfair dismissal was out of time. [1974] I.C.R. 53.

Commentary

Thus, the court held, money in lieu of notice did not extend the EDT beyond the time when the actual employment ceased.

Adams v GKN Sankey Ltd 1980

The employee's employment was terminated by the employer by letter on November 2, 1979. The letter stated that the employee was given 12 weeks' notice from November 5, but that she was not required to work the notice period and would receive money in lieu of notice. The employee complained on February 22, 1980 of unfair dismissal, but the tribunal ruled that the claim was out of time because her employment had terminated on November 5, 1979.

Held: (EAT) The court distinguished between the situation in *Dedman*, where, they claimed, employment had been terminated immediately, but monies had been paid in lieu of notice, and the present case. In the instant case the letter terminating the employment stated, in effect, that the employment would be terminated 12 weeks from the date of the letter, and that the monies paid were in lieu of her having to work the notice period. Thus the claim for unfair dismissal had been made in time. [1980] I.R.L.R. 416.

Commentary
This may appear to be something of an artificial distinction between monies paid instead of giving notice (*Dedman*), and monies paid instead of requiring the employee to work out the given notice period (*Adams*). It certainly places significance on the actual wording used by the employer when terminating the employment.

Robert Cort & Son Ltd v Charman 1981
The employee's contract of employment provided for one month's notice of termination. On September 24, 1980 he was advised that his employment would cease on September 26, 1980. On September 26 he received a letter stating that his employment was terminated as from September 26, 1980 and that he would receive one month's money in lieu of notice. At the time it was necessary for an employee to have 52 weeks continuous employment in order to qualify for a complaint of unfair dismissal. If the EDT was September 26 he would be unable to make a claim for unfair dismissal, but if the employment had not terminated until October 26 he would be eligible.

Held: (EAT) The Court of Appeal decision in *Dedman* was binding authority that in a case of immediate dismissal where money is paid in lieu of notice, the EDT is the date of the dismissal, and not the date on which the notice period would expire. The employment was thus terminated on September 26 and Mr Charman was not entitled to bring a claim of unfair dismissal. [1981] I.R.L.R. 437.

Commentary
The court did, however, make the point *obiter* that it would still be open to the employee to bring a common law action for breach of contract, and, if successful, damages may include the loss of the right to complain of unfair dismissal.

Stapp v The Shaftsbury Society 1982
On January 24, 1980 Mr Stapp was given one month's notice of termination of his employment. Since he had started work on February 26, 1979, Mr Stapp would therefore be eligible to make a claim for unfair dismissal. Mr Stapp then commenced both the employer's internal grievance procedure and also proceedings for unfair dismissal. On February 7, 1980 his employer wrote requiring Mr Stapp to leave immediately with a cheque for monies up to February 23. When the tribunal hearing

commenced, the employer argued that Mr Stapp did not have the 52 weeks continuity of employment required, since his employment had been terminated before February 23, 1980. The tribunal agreed with the employer, and on appeal the EAT held that Mr Stapp's employment had been terminated on February 7.

Held: (CA) Despite the fact that the employee was already under notice of dismissal, the effect of the letter of February 7 was to immediately terminate the contract of employment; consequently, the EDT was February 7, 1980, and Mr Stapp did not have sufficient continuity of employment to apply for unfair dismissal. [1982] I.R.L.R. 326.

Commentary

The court made a number of other points: Firstly, that it was possible for the employer to dismiss summarily, even though the employee might already be under notice of dismissal. Secondly, in such a case, the EDT would be the date on which the employment actually came to an end. Finally, should Mr Stapp bring an action for breach of the employment contract, damages sought may include the loss of right to complain of unfair dismissal.

Batchelor v British Railways Board 1987

Following relatively minor disciplinary charges, Miss Batchelor was dismissed with immediate effect on February 5, 1985. She immediately appealed against the decision, using the employer's grievance procedure. On February 25 she was informed that the appeal had been unsuccessful. On May 13, 1985 her complaint of unfair dismissal was received by the tribunal. The employer argued that as her termination of employment took place on February 5, her unfair dismissal complaint was out of the three month time limit imposed by what is now s.111 of the Employment Rights Act 1996. The tribunal, however, held that her termination was effective only on February 25, and this decision was upheld by the EAT.

Held: (CA) The court held that the EDT was February 5, 1985, and the effect of a clear notice of termination could not be altered by the fact that the employer may have operated the disciplinary procedure improperly. [1987] I.R.L.R. 136.

Commentary

The requirements of s.111 of the ERA 1996 are strictly observed by the courts (see above), so it is essential that the EDT be correctly identified, since failure to do so may in some cases restrict the employee to an action only for wrongful dismissal.

Key Principle: **The three-month time limit imposed under s.111 of the ERA 1996 is strictly applied.**

Norgett v Luton Industrial Co-op Society Ltd 1976

The employee was charged with theft from his employer and dismissed on November 25, 1974. On May 22, 1975 he was acquitted of theft, and immediately complained of unfair dismissal. The tribunal found that his complaint had not been made within the three-month time limit, and declined to hear it.

Held: (EAT) Although, naturally, the issue of guilt or innocence was of prime importance to the employee, it was still "reasonably practicable" for him to have brought his complaint within the three-month time limit. Since he had failed to do so, the tribunal were correct to hold that they had no jurisdiction to hear the complaint. [1976] I.C.R. 442.

Commentary

The case was heard shortly after the time scale for presentation of complaints had been extended from four weeks to three months. Perhaps, therefore, the court was unwilling to be seen to be extending a time frame which had only recently been tripled from one to three months.

Riley v Tesco Stores Ltd 1980

Ms Riley was dismissed on October 6, 1976 on suspicion of theft. She consulted a Citizens Advice Bureau about a claim for unfair dismissal, but was apparently advised that she should wait until after criminal proceedings had been heard. On August 4, 1977 she was acquitted of criminal charges, and sought to bring a complaint of unfair dismissal. The tribunal held that Ms Riley's complaint had been presented outside the three-month time limit, and thus the tribunal had no jurisdiction to hear it. The decision was upheld by the EAT.

Held: (CA) The issue in question was whether it was "reasonably practicable" for the complaint to have been made within the three-month period. Reliance on possibly incorrect advice from a third party may be a factor for consideration, but in this case the tribunal were entitled to find as a question of fact that it had been reasonably practicable for Ms Riley to bring her complaint within the permitted time scale. [1980] I.C.R. 323.

Commentary

Although the court has authority to extend the time scale in cases where it considers that it was not reasonably practicable for the complaint to have been presented within the three-month period (s.111(2)(b) of the ERA 1996), the courts have interpreted the section strictly.

Identifying a Dismissal

Key Principle: **It is sometimes necessary to look beyond the actual words or actions in order to determine whether a dismissal has taken place.**

S Futty v D & D Brekkes Ltd 1974

Mr Futty had been employed for some five years as a fish filleter on Hull Docks. On the occasion in question, some banter between employees, including the applicant, had turned acrimonious. At one stage the foreman turned to the applicant and said: "If you do not like the job, fuck off." The applicant left the firm, found another job and claimed he had been dismissed for the purpose of unfair dismissal. Evidence was presented to the tribunal that such language was occasionally used on the docks, but it meant nothing more than "you can leave your work, clock off, and you will be paid up to the time when you do so. Then you can come back when you are disposed to start work again the next day." Furthermore, other employees had assumed that Mr Futty had merely gone of in a "huff" and would be returning the following day.

Held: (IT) The tribunal found that, in the fish trade, once the question of dismissal becomes imminent, bad language disappears and the parties adopt a formal approach, indicating in this case that it was not the intention or true understanding of the parties that a dismissal had taken place. Further, the tribunal found that had the applicant not been successful in obtaining another job, he would have returned and resumed his old job. For these reasons, no dismissal had taken place. [1974] I.R.L.R. 130.

Commentary
Obviously, the use of similar language in a different work situation may well lead to a different conclusion.

Martin v Yeoman Aggregates Ltd 1983
Mr Martin worked as transport manager for the employer. On one occasion he obtained an incorrect part for one of the company vehicles; this led to an argument between him and one of the directors, during which Mr Martin refused to go and get the correct part, and the director responded by dismissing him. Within five minutes the director realised that the dismissal was in contravention of the company's disciplinary procedure, and he therefore advised Mr Martin that he was suspended without pay for two days whilst the disciplinary process was followed. This was supported by a letter from the personnel manager. Mr Martin, however, took the view that he had been dismissed and applied to a tribunal for a finding of unfair dismissal.

Held: (EAT) The decision of the tribunal that Mr Martin had not been dismissed was upheld. Despite the fact that unambiguous words had been used, they were withdrawn almost immediately. Furthermore, it is a matter of common sense that either the employer or the employee should be given an opportunity of resiling from words used in the heat of the moment. [1983] I.R.L.R. 49.

Commentary
A common sense decision, but bear in mind that the duty of mutual trust and confidence has greatly increased in scope since this decision was reached. Could it therefore now be argued that the mere speaking of the words, particularly if in front of a third party, would have the effect of breaching mutual trust and confidence, and thus giving rise to a claim of constructive dismissal and bringing the relationship to an end?

Birch and Humber v The University of Liverpool 1985
The applicants were members of the university staff. In 1982 the university announced a need to cut back on staff, but hoped to do this by offering staff an early retirement scheme rather than by way of redundancy. The applicants took advantage of the

early retirement scheme, but then applied to a tribunal on the grounds that they had been dismissed by reason of redundancy.

Held: (CA) The court found that the applicants' employment had not been terminated by dismissal on the grounds of redundancy, but by mutual agreement. They stated that a finding of redundancy would not be appropriate in situations where the termination was brought about either by the employee or by freely given mutual consent. [1985] I.C.R. 470.

Commentary
On the facts of this case, the decision appears very fair—perhaps the applicants were trying to "have their cake and eat it" by claiming not only monies under the early retirement scheme but also redundancy payments. However, there is perhaps in some situations a very fine dividing line between agreement brought about by coercion, which the court stressed would not amount to true mutual consent, and freely given mutual consent.

Key Principle: **On occasion it may be possible to claim for unfair dismissal whilst remaining in employment.**

Hogg v Dover College 1990
The applicant was a teacher and department head, who, following time off through illness, returned to work on a part-time basis. The employer wrote to Mr Hogg stating that due to his ill health it would not be possible for him to continue as department head, and his teaching hours and salary would be substantially reduced. Mr Hogg responded that the letter amounted to a dismissal, but that pending a hearing from a tribunal for unfair dismissal he would continue working on the terms offered.

Held: (EAT) The letter from the employer had terminated the contract of employment and therefore Mr Hogg had been dismissed. Alternatively, the letter had substantially changed the terms of his employment contract and entitled Mr Hogg to resign and claim constructive dismissal. The fact that he chose to continue working did not have the effect of confirming and accepting the changes, since his continued employment was under a totally different contract. [1990] I.C.R. 39.

Commentary
It is not yet clear how far this approach may be taken—when does a change to the contractual terms and conditions allow an

employee to both claim unfair dismissal and remain in employment?

Alcan Extrusions v Yates 1996

For economic reasons and following failure between the employer and the trade unions to agree, the employer introduced new shift patterns and working hours into the employment contracts of its workforce. This had a detrimental effect on the employees' overtime payments, shift allowance payments and holiday date choice. The employees claimed that the changes amounted to a dismissal, but that they would continue to work under the new system pending an application to a tribunal for unfair dismissal and/or redundancy.

Held: (EAT) Where the employer unilaterally imposes radically different terms of employment, following the decision in *Hogg*, there is a dismissal, and that dismissal is not affected by the employee choosing to remain working, under protest, under the new conditions. [1996] I.R.L.R. 327.

Commentary

The court also made the point that whether the new terms imposed were so radically different so as to amount to the removal of the old contract and the substitution of a new inferior contract, was a question of fact and degree to be decided by the tribunal on the facts of each individual case.

Key Principle: **Since statute deems that the non-renewal of a fixed term contract gives rise to a dismissal, it is necessary to differentiate between fixed term and other contracts.**

Brown v Knowsley Borough Council 1986

The applicant had been employed as a temporary teacher on a series of fixed term contracts between 1979 and 1984. The employment was made possible through a grant from the Manpower Services Commission, and the employment contract contained a term that the appointment would only last for as long as funding was available. In 1984 the contract was not renewed because funding was no longer available from the MSC. The applicant claimed a redundancy payment—which would only be available if a dismissal had taken place.

Held: (EAT) The court considered the argument that the contract was a fixed task, rather than a fixed term, contract—automatically ending when the specific task of teaching had ended each year, and not therefore giving rise to a dismissal. However, the preferred view was that it was neither a fixed term nor a fixed task contract, but a contract automatically terminating on the happening or non-happening of a future event; again not giving rise to a dismissal. [1986] I.R.L.R. 102.

Commentary
Although no distinction is made between fixed term contracts, fixed task contracts, and contracts determinable upon the happening or non-happening of some future event, for the purpose of the Fixed-term Employees (Prevention of Less Favourable Treatment) Regulations 2002, for other purposes it *may* be necessary to distinguish between them.

Key Principle: **Where the employee commits a repudiatory breach of the employment contract, the contract is actually terminated by the employer's acceptance of that breach, and thus a dismissal takes place.**

London Transport Executive v Clarke 1981
The employee took seven weeks unauthorised leave of absence from his work. After the first four weeks the employer wrote to him to say that he was no longer on their books for employment. The employee sought to prove that he had been dismissed in order to claim for unfair dismissal.

Held: (CA) The majority decision of the court was that "the acceptance by an employer of repudiation by a worker who wishes to continue his employment notwithstanding his repudiatory conduct constitutes the determination of the contract of employment by the employer;"—*per* Templeman L.J. [1981] I.C.R. 355.

Commentary
This is not, of course, to say that the dismissal is unfair; merely that a dismissal has taken place.

Igbo v Johnson Matthey Chemicals Ltd [1986]
The applicant wished to take extended annual leave in order to visit her family in Nigeria. The employer agreed providing that

she sign an agreement that should she not return by the agreed date her employment would automatically terminate. On her return to the UK Mrs Igbo was ill and did not return to work by the agreed date. Her employer treated the employment contract as having been automatically terminated and no dismissal having taken place.

Held: (CA) The court took the view that the agreement was contrary to (what is now) s.203 of the Employment Rights Act 1996, which states that any provision which seeks either to limit the provisions of the ERA, or seeks to preclude anyone from bringing an action under ERA, shall be void. Thus in this case the agreement could not stand and a dismissal had taken place. [1986] I.R.L.R. 215.

Commentary
The court felt that general acceptance of such clauses could be very harsh to the employees; they suggested an example whereby an employee with an impeccable record was returning to work on time as agreed, but was knocked down by a car a matter of feet from the employer's works. If he managed to crawl inside the gate, he would presumably be entitled to time off sick; whereas, if he did not manage to get inside the gate, his contract may be automatically terminated. It may be interesting to compare such a situation with either the doctrine of frustration or the decision in *Brown v Knowsley*.

Key Principle: **Termination by mutual consent is very rarely established by the courts.**

SW Strange Ltd v Mann 1965
Mr Mann was employed as a manager under an employment contract which contained a restraint of trade clause. Following disagreements, both parties agreed that he should relinquish his present job and take up a different post within the company. His new contract of employment did not contain the restrictive covenant. When he was dismissed from the company a short time later, the company sought to enforce the restraint clause against him.

Held: (ChD) The clause could not be enforced, since the original contract had been terminated by mutual agreement, and the clause was not present in the new contract. [1965 1 All E.R. 1069.

Commentary
The case is usually cited in respect of restraint of trade clauses, but it is one of the few in which the courts have found termination of the employment contract by mutual consent.

Scott v Coalite Fuels & Chemicals Ltd 1988
Following a downturn in business, the employer decided it was necessary to make a number of redundancies. Those employees selected were given a number of options which included an early retirement package, as an alternative to redundancy. The applicant chose the early retirement package, but then submitted a claim for a redundancy payment.

Held: (EAT) The EAT upheld the decision of the tribunal that the applicant had terminated his own employment by choosing to accept an early retirement package, and that since no dismissal had therefore taken place, there could be no claim for redundancy. [1988] I.C.R. 355.

Commentary
The court also held that although selection for redundancy had taken place and been notified some months before the early retirement scheme had been offered or accepted, the acceptance of early retirement had effectively superceded the redundancy notice. See also the case of *Birch v University of Liverpool*.

Constructive Dismissal

Key Principle: **"... an employee is dismissed by his employer if ... the employee terminates the contract under which he is employed (with or without notice) in circumstances in which he is entitled to terminate it without notice by reason of the employer's conduct." (s.95(1)(c) of the ERA 1996).**

Western Excavating (ECC) Ltd v Sharp 1978
Mr Sharp, having worked some hours overtime, asked for time off in lieu, a common and agreed practice within the company.

Unfortunately the company was particularly busy, and his request for time off was refused. Nevertheless, Mr Sharp took the time off. On his return the following day, Mr Sharp was dismissed for failing to carry out a reasonable order. The dismissal was reversed by the company's disciplinary hearing, and a penalty of five days suspension without pay was substituted. Mr Sharp thus found himself short of money and requested a loan from the company, which was refused. He then requested that he be allowed to draw against his accrued holiday pay, which was also refused as being against company policy. He then apparently decided that his only option was to get hold of his holiday pay, which he did by resigning. He received the monies owing to him and immediately made a complaint to the industrial tribunal of unfair dismissal. The tribunal apparently found that the company had acted unreasonably, and this justified the actions of Mr Sharp. Owing to conflicting *dicta* the EAT felt unable to disturb the findings of the tribunal.

Held: (CA) Lord Denning M.R. considered the two options: the contract test and the unreasonableness test. The contract test holds that for the employee to leave and claim constructive dismissal, the employer must have committed a fundamental breach of the contract or have evinced a clear intention not to be bound by one or more of the essential conditions of the contract. The unreasonableness test, however, states that if the employer acts so unreasonably that the employee cannot fairly be expected to put up with it any longer, then the employee is entitled to leave and claim a dismissal. Lord Denning argued in favour of the contract test, citing both the words of the statute and the benefit of the certainty of a contract test rather than the "whimsical" approach of a test of reasonableness. In this case, therefore, as the employers were not in breach of any fundamental contractual terms, there was no dismissal. [1978] Q.B. 761.

Commentary
Recent developments in the duty of mutual trust and confidence have caused some commentators to suggest a reintroduction of the unreasonableness test "by the back door". By invoking a contract term, the employer cannot—under the contract test—be in breach of that term; but the *manner* in which he invokes it may breach the term of duty of mutual trust and confidence (see, *e.g. United Bank v Akhtar* and *Woods v WM Car Services*).

Savoia v Chiltern Herb Farms Ltd 1981
Mr Savoia was the supervisor in the packing department. Whilst he was off sick his work was handled by another employee. The employer found the other employee to be more co-operative than Mr Savoia, so when he returned to work Mr Savoia was offered a different job within the company, which he refused, apparently on unsubstantiated medical grounds. As he was not allowed to return to his old job, Mr Savoia left and made a complaint of unfair dismissal through constructive dismissal.

Held: (EAT) Mr Savoia had been constructively dismissed, however, on the particular facts of the case, the dismissal was not unfair. [1981] I.R.L.R. 65.

Commentary
Generally a finding of constructive dismissal will lead to a finding that the dismissal was unfair. This is one of the few cases which demonstrates that a finding of constructive dismissal does nothing more than prove that a dismissal has taken place, and is properly nothing more than one step in the process of an unfair dismissal claim.

Potentially Fair Reasons for Dismissal

Key Principle: **Statute has identified five potentially fair reasons for dismissal: capability or qualifications; conduct; redundancy; contravention of a statute; some other substantial reason.**

Taylor v Alidair Ltd 1978
Mr Taylor was a commercial pilot. On one occasion he made a bad landing, damaging the aeroplane but causing no injury to any of the passengers on board. Following an inquiry he was dismissed. He claimed unfair dismissal.

Held: (CA)

"There are activities in which the degree of professional skill which must be required is so high, and the potential consequences of the smallest departure from that high standard are so serious, that one failure to perform in accordance with those standards is enough to justify the dismissal." *Per* Lord Denning M.R. [1978] I.R.L.R. 82.

Commentary
In most instances of mistake, a series of verbal or written warnings, or a period of retraining would probably be the appropriate response.

International Sports Co Ltd v Thompson 1980
In her last 18 months of employment with International Sports, Ms Thompson was off sick for a total of some five months. Her medical certificates ranged from dizzy spells to viral infections and flatulence. In agreement with her trade union the company issued a series of warnings to her, and reviewed her medical history which consisted of a series of unrelated, transitory complaints. She was finally dismissed for her unsatisfactory performance. She complained of unfair dismissal.

Held: (EAT) The dismissal was fair. The company had carried out reasonable investigation into her absences, given her an opportunity to respond, issued warnings, and in the absence of any improvement in her attendance, were justified in dismissing her. [1980] I.R.L.R. 340.

Commentary
Much of the previous case law concerned employees dismissed for absence due to serious and prolonged illness. Although this case was considered on the grounds of conduct, in cases such as this dismissal will normally be on the grounds of capability—since the employer would probably not wish to prove that the employee was actually malingering.

RS Components Ltd v Irwin 1973
Mr Irwin was a salesman for an electronics components supplier. He was offered a new contract of employment including a restrictive covenant to the effect that he would not solicit any of his employer's customers for a period of 12 months after leaving his present employment. He was also told that if he refused to sign he would be dismissed. Mr Irwin did refuse to sign and was dismissed. He then brought a complaint for unfair dismissal.

Held: (NIRC) The category of "some other substantial reason" is deliberately wide and should not be construed *ejusdem generis* with the other categories listed. [1973] I.C.R. 535.

Commentary
At first instance the tribunal had held that Mr Irwin had been unfairly dismissed, since the reason for his dismissal did not appear

to be in a similar category to the other reasons listed in statute. The NIRC and later courts have made it clear that the category of "some other substantial reason" is not a closed category, consequently it has become something of a "catch-all" or "dustbin" category.

Hollister v National Farmers' Union 1979

Mr Hollister was employed by the NFU in Cornwall, where for historical reasons employment conditions with the NFU were different from other parts of the country. It was decided to bring employees in Cornwall in line with other areas by changing various terms and conditions within the employment contract. Most of the changes had beneficial, rather than adverse effects, on the employees, but the pension arrangements were not as good. Mr Hollister refused to accept the changes, and the employer dismissed him. He brought a claim of unfair dismissal.

Held: (CA) A properly consulted-upon reorganisation, brought about for sound, good business reasons would be a substantial reason of a kind sufficient to justify a dismissal of this kind. [1979] I.R.L.R. 238.

Commentary

This decision and those which have followed it give considerable scope to employers to make unilateral changes to employees' contracts of employment; on the one hand is the supposed "sanctity of the contract", whilst on the other is the implied duty of the employee to adapt.

Saunders v Scottish National Camps Association Ltd (1981)

Mr Saunders worked as a maintenance handyman at a camp used by large numbers of schoolchildren and teenagers. He was dismissed by his employer, the reason given was that he indulged in homosexuality. Psychiatric evidence was given that Mr Saunders represented no danger to children, and that in the view of the psychiatrist homosexuals were no more likely to interfere with children than were heterosexuals. The tribunal found, however, that a large body of employers would wish to restrict the employment of a homosexual in such circumstances, and held therefore that the dismissal on the grounds of "some other substantial reason" was fair.

Held: (CS) The Court of Sessions upheld the finding of the EAT that the tribunal had been entitled to find the dismissal fair falling, as it did, within the "band of reasonable responses" test (see *Iceland Frozen Foods v Jones*). [1981] I.R.L.R. 277.

Commentary
The decision, though perhaps not rational, and possibly now falling foul of issues under the Human Rights Act 1998, does indicate both the scope of the category of "some other substantial reason" and issues raised as to the application of the "band of reasonable responses" test when considering the fairness of a dismissal.

The Fairness of the Dismissal

Key Principle: **The fairness of the dismissal depends upon whether the employer acted reasonably or unreasonably in treating the reason as a sufficient reason for dismissal, and that shall be determined in accordance with equity and the substantial merits of the case.**

Iceland Frozen Foods Ltd v Jones 1982
The employee worked on the night shift and was dismissed for failing to operate a security system and for attempting to deceive the employer into making additional overtime payments. He made a claim for unfair dismissal. The tribunal found that the conduct of the employee was not sufficiently serious as to warrant dismissal, and thus the dismissal was unfair.

Held: (EAT) The correct approach for the tribunal was to consider whether the employer's decision to dismiss the employee fell within the band of reasonable responses which a reasonable employer could adopt—if it did, the dismissal was fair. [1983] I.C.R. 17.

Commentary
The tribunal must not, therefore, ask: "What would we have done?" but rather: "Could a reasonable employer have acted as this employer did?"

Haddon v Van Den Bergh Foods Ltd

Mr Haddon had been employed for 15 years and was due to receive a good service award at a presentation ceremony. His supervisor had advised him that following the ceremony he should return to complete his shift. At the ceremony Mr Haddon drank alcohol and decided that he should not return to his place of work. He was dismissed for failing to carry out a lawful order, even though it was accepted that his absence had made no difference to the productivity of his shift. He complained of unfair dismissal. The tribunal applied the test of "range of reasonable responses", and concluded that it could not be said that *no* reasonable employer would have dismissed Mr Haddon. Therefore the dismissal could not be found to be unfair.

Held: (EAT) The EAT argued that the test of "band of reasonable responses" was, in effect, a test of perversity, and held that the correct approach was to consider the words of the statute and consider the case on its merits in accordance with the principles of equity. [1999] I.R.L.R. 672.

Commentary

In many respects this is a very attractive argument. The use of the "band of reasonable responses" test has made it very difficult for an employee to prove an unfair dismissal. The test has often been taken to require that unless a tribunal is able to state that no reasonable employer could have taken the decision made, the dismissal will be fair. This appears to go beyond what is required by statute. The reasoning from *Hadden* was fully endorsed by the EAT in *Wilson v Ethicon Ltd* [2000] I.R.L.R. 4, but firmly disapproved by the Court of Appeal in the following joined cases of *Foley* and *Madden*.

Foley v Post Office : HSBC Bank plc (formerly Midland Bank plc) v Madden 2000

Both cases concerned issues of unfair dismissal. In the case of *Foley*, the issue was whether the EAT were entitled to substitute their own decision for that of the tribunal, rather than allowing that on the basis of the facts the tribunal were justified in finding that the employer had acted reasonably in treating the reason for the dismissal as a sufficient reason.

In *Madden* the issue was two-fold. Firstly, the EAT had attempted to restrict the effect of *Hadden* by stating that the test of "band of reasonable responses" should be applied in conjunction with the actual words of the statute. Unfortunately, the EAT then went on to suggest that the three stage test from *BHS v Burchell* related solely to the reason for the dismissal rather than to the reasonableness of the decision.

Held: (CA) The Court of Appeal gave an authoritative statement that the "band or range of reasonable responses" approach as detailed in *Iceland Frozen Foods v Jones* [1983] I.C.R. 17 remained binding, and that the approach of the EAT in *Hadden* formed "an unwarranted departure from binding authority". Furthermore, the suggestion by the EAT that the test from *BHS v Burchell* related to the reason rather than the reasonableness, was inconsistent with binding authority. [2000] I.R.L.R. 827.

Commentary
This judgment is welcomed in as far as it provides certainty into the issue of use of the "band of reasonable responses" test, doubted in *Hadden* and others. However, some may feel that strict application of the test may indeed amount to the application of a "test of perversity", as indeed did the court in *Hadden*.

Key Principle: **Multiple dismissals may be fair, even if the employer has no belief in the "wrongdoing" of the employee.**

Monie v Coral Racing Ltd 1981
Money was discovered to be missing from a safe to which only two people, the appellant and his assistant, held a key. An investigation was undertaken and the firm's security officer concluded that either the appellant or his assistant must be guilty—there was, however, no way of determining which. The employer dismissed both employees.

Held: (CA) "... where there is a reasonable suspicion that one of two or possibly both employees must have acted dishonestly it is not necessary for the employer to believe that either of them acted dishonestly."—*per* Dunn L.J. [1981] I.C.R. 109.

Commentary
This principle has since been extended beyond instances of dishonesty, to a case of negligence in *McPhie v Wimpey Waste Manage-*

ment Ltd [1981] I.R.L.R. 316, a case of capability in *Whitbread & Co plc v Thomas* [1988] I.R.L.R. 43, and a case concerning one of a group of four suspected in *Parr v Whitbread & Co plc* [1990] I.C.R. 427.

Key Principle: **It has been possible for a dismissal for a fair reason, which was within the band of reasonable responses, to be found to be unfair if it failed the test of procedural fairness.**

Polkey v AE Dayton Services Ltd 1988

Mr Polkey was one of four van drivers. The company decided to replace the drivers with two van salespeople, and since only one of the existing van drivers was considered suitable, it was decided to make the other three redundant. Without any prior consultation, warning or notice, Mr Polkey was called into the office, informed of his redundancy and sent home. He submitted a claim for unfair dismissal. The tribunal followed the principle from *British Labour Pump v Byrne* and held that since prior consultation would have made no difference, the dismissal was fair. This decision was supported by the EAT and the Court of Appeal.

Held: (HL) The principal as stated in *British Labour Pump* was no longer good law. A fair procedure should be adopted by the employer in all cases unless there were reasonable grounds for the employer to believe that such procedure would have been "utterly useless". [1988] I.C.R. 142.

Commentary

The old approach from *British Labour Pump* was to ask whether adopting the correct procedure *would have made* any difference. Following *Polkey*, the failure by an employer to adopt the correct procedure should lead to a finding of unfair dismissal, but it appears that the courts are sometimes willing to adopt a forgiving approach towards the employer if the overall procedure is not unfair (see for example *Eclipse Blinds v Wright* [1992] I.R.L.R. 133).

The newly introduced s.98A of the Employment Rights Act 1996 states that if the employer fails to complete the procedure laid down in the Statutory Dispute Resolution Procedures contained in Sch.2, Pt I of the Employment Act 2002, the resulting dismissal will be unfair. However, s.98A(2) then states:

> (2) Subject to subsection(1), failure by an employer to follow a procedure in relation to dismissal of an employee shall not be regarded for the purposes of section 98(4)(a) as by itself making the employer's action unreasonable if he shows that he would have decided to dismiss the employee if he had followed the procedure.

Key Principle: **Only those issues known to the employer at the time of the dismissal may be taken into account when assessing the fairness of the dismissal.**

W Devis & Sons Ltd v Atkins 1977

Mr Atkins was employed as abattoir manager. Part of his duties involved him buying animals. The company repeatedly instructed him to buy direct from farmers, but he persisted in buying from dealers. He was dismissed and complained of unfair dismissal. At the tribunal hearing the company sought to introduce evidence that had been gained after Mr Atkins' dismissal to the effect that he had been receiving secret commission from the dealers. The question for the court was whether information may be relied upon within the hearing that was not known at the time of the dismissal.

Held: (HL) Referring to the words of the statute (now s.98(4) of the ERA 1996), the House was unable to accept that the tribunal may have regard to matters of which the employer was unaware when dismissing the employee, in order to determine whether the employer's reasons were fair or not. [1977] A.C. 931.

Commentary

In other words, only those facts believed or known by the employer at the time of making the decision to dismiss may be considered by the tribunal in seeking to determine the fairness of the employer's actions.

West Midland Co-operative Society Ltd v Tipton 1986

Mr Tipton was summarily dismissed on account of his particularly poor attendance record. The employer then refused to allow him to appeal against his dismissal, contrary to the company's agreed disciplinary procedure. Mr Tipton complained of unfair dismissal. The tribunal found the dismissal unfair and the EAT upheld their findings. The Court of Appeal, however, apparently followed *Devis v Atkins*, and held that the tribunal should not take into account matters happening or coming to light after the actual dismissal.

Held: (HL) Their Lordships adopted an equitable approach to the problem. On the one hand, a dismissal is unfair if the employer unreasonably treats his real reason as a sufficient reason to dismiss either at the time of the dismissal or during the course of a disciplinary or appeal hearing. At the same time, a dismissal may be unfair if the employee is denied a contractual right of appeal, and thereby denied the opportunity of showing that in the circumstances the employer's reason for dismissal could not be reasonably seen as sufficient. On the facts of this case, the appeal was allowed. [1986] A.C. 536.

Commentary

The case may appear to demonstrate an apparent inconsistency: if the tribunal may not consider matters not known at the time of the dismissal, and if the dismissal takes place prior to an appeal or disciplinary hearing, the tribunal should not consider matters arising from the hearing. Perhaps the simplest way of considering the matter is to remember that if the employee is contractually entitled to a disciplinary hearing, and if that hearing is withheld from the employee, there would appear *prima facie* to be strong grounds for an unfair dismissal finding.

British Home Stores Ltd v Burchell 1978

Ms Burchell was dismissed because the employer believed she was stealing from a staff discount scheme. She complained of unfair dismissal. The tribunal found the dismissal to be fair, but this was reversed on appeal to the EAT.

Held: (EAT) The EAT laid down a three stage procedure:

(a) that the employer honestly held the belief;

(b) that the employer had reasonable grounds on which to sustain the belief; and

(c) that the employer had carried out as much investigation as was reasonable in all the circumstances. [1978] I.R.L.R. 379.

Commentary
It is important to note that the question for the tribunal does not concern the guilt or innocence of the applicant, but the question of whether in view of the facts as they were known to the employer at the time, the employer acted reasonably both in the decision and the manner of the dismissal.

The *Burchell* approach has since been approved by the Court of Appeal in the case of *W Weddel & Co Ltd v Tepper* [1980] I.C.R. 286, but the EAT in *Boys and Girls Welfare Society v McDonald* [1996] I.R.L.R. 129 warned against an over-simplistic use of the *Burchell* formula, although the test was again cited with approval by the Court of Sessions in *Scottish Daily Record and Sunday Mail v Laird* [1996] I.R.L.R. 665.

10. REDUNDANCY

Key Principle: **Although redundancy is defined in s.139 of the Employment Rights Act 1996, two issues have given rise to problems: what is meant by "work of a particular kind" and "place of work".**

"Work of a particular kind"

North Riding Garages Ltd v Butterwick 1967
Mr Butterwick had for some 30 years worked at North Riding Garages, for much of the time as a mechanic, but in later years as workshop manager. Despite his job title he still spent much time working as a hands-on mechanic rather than in a purely management role. When new owners took over they required him to spend more time on sales and paperwork, which Mr Butterwick was not able to do satisfactorily. After some months he was dismissed. He claimed that he was redundant.

Held: (QBD) Employees have a duty to adapt to new methods and techniques; only if the new methods alter the nature of the work required may they be classed as redundant. In this case, the function of workshop manager remained, thus Mr Butterwick was not redundant. [1967] 2 Q.B. 56.

Commentary
This may be seen as an example of the "function test" in defining "work of a particular kind". The court is called upon to consider whether the overall function of the role—rather than the specific work detailed in the employment contract—had changed.

Nelson v BBC 1980
The employee had been employed as a producer and editor for the BBC. For most of his time he had worked on the Caribbean Service. When the Caribbean Service was closed down, the question arose as to whether Mr Nelson was redundant.

Held: (CA) Although there had been a diminution of the specific work Mr Nelson had been doing, there had been no such diminution in the work of producers and editors generally within the BBC. Since Mr Nelson had been employed as a producer and editor, and not specifically as a producer and editor on the Caribbean Service, it could not be said that there had been a diminution in the work which he was contracted to do. Thus, he was not redundant. [1980] I.C.R. 100.

Commentary
An example of the "contract test" in defining "work of a particular kind". The court looked not at what the employee actually did, but at what he was contracted to do.

Safeway Stores plc v Burrell 1997
Mr Burrell was employed as a petrol station manager. The company decided to reorganise the management structure by doing away with the position of petrol station manager and creating the post of petrol filling station controller. All petrol station managers were made redundant and invited to apply for one of the new positions, which carried a lower salary and differed to an extent in job description. Mr Burrell decided not to apply for one of the new posts and accepted the redundancy. He then complained of unfair dismissal, arguing that the new post was identical to his old job and therefore he was not redundant.

Held: (EAT) Neither the use of a "function test" nor a "contract test" was appropriate. The correct approach requires a three-stage process: (1) was the employee dismissed? If so, (2) had the requirements of the employer's business for employees to carry out work of a particular kind ceased or diminished, or were they expected to cease or diminish? If so, (3) was the dismissal of the employee caused wholly or mainly by that state of affairs? [1997] I.C.R. 523.

Commentary
This "statutory approach" by the EAT also allows for the principle of "bumped" redundancy, whereby an employee may be redundant, not because his own job is redundant, but because his job has been filled by another employee who would himself otherwise have been made redundant.

Murray v Foyle Meats Ltd 1999
Mr Murray was employed as a meat plant operative, working almost exclusively in the company's slaughter hall, although his contract of employment required him to work in any part of the employer's operation. Because of a decrease in work, the company required fewer employees in the slaughter hall and selected a number of employees, including Mr Murray, from amongst those employed in the slaughter hall, for redundancy. Mr Murray argued that, since his contract required him to work in any area of the operation, to select only from those workers actually working in the slaughter hall was unfair, and he complained of unfair dismissal. In effect, he argued that the court should apply the "contract test", and the company argued that the "function test" should be applied.

Held: (HL) Both the contract test and the function test "missed the point". The correct approach was to apply the words of the statute and ask whether the dismissals were "attributable" to the diminution in work. In this case they were, thus Mr Murray was redundant. [1999] I.C.R. 827.

Commentary
This is an important case. It effectively disapproves the use of both the "contract test" and the "function test" in determining "work of a particular kind", and approves the statutory approach taken in *Safeway Stores v Burrell*. It also, therefore, allows for the principle of "bumped" redundancies.

"Place of work"

High Table Ltd v Horst 1997
Ms Horst had worked for High Table, a catering company, as a

waitress for a number of years at the premises of one of their clients, Hill Samuel, in the City of London. Following a down-turn in the business between High Table and Hill Samuel in 1993, Ms Horst was made redundant. She argued that since her employment contract contained an express mobility clause—which purported to allow the employer to transfer staff on a temporary or permanent basis to any location—her "place of work" was at any of her employer's clients, and not just at Hill Samuels. She maintained that she could and should have been offered work elsewhere, thus was not redundant, and claimed unfair dismissal.

Held: (CA) The Court of Appeal rejected her argument, coming down in favour of a factual approach, and stating: "If an employee has worked in only one location under his contract of employment ... it defies common sense to widen the extent of the place where he was so employed, merely because of the existence of a mobility clause. Of course, the refusal by the employee to obey a lawful requirement under the contract of employment to move may constitute a valid reason for dismissal, but issues of dismissal, redundancy and reasonableness in the actions of an employer should be kept distinct."—*per* Peter Gibson L.J. [1997] I.R.L.R. 513.

Commentary
Presumably therefore, place of work is factual. It is, of course, necessary to bear in mind *dicta* from *Murray* which states that if the dismissal is attributable to a redundancy situation, the dismissal is by reason of redundancy. On the other hand, if the employee has a mobility clause in his contract of employment and the employer chooses to transfer him to another location rather than to declare him redundant, this will, following *Western Excavating*, be lawful; unless either the reason for the transfer or the manner of the transfer breach the implied duty of mutual trust and confidence, in which case it may lead to unfair dismissal (*United Bank v Akhtar*).

Key Principle: **It is important for an employer to follow a procedure of good industrial practice to ensure that a redundancy does not amount to an unfair dismissal.**

Williams v Compare Maxam Ltd 1982
The company needed to make a number of redundancies, and called for employees to apply for voluntary redundancy.

However, insufficient numbers of employees applied, and a number of compulsory redundancies were necessary. No prior consultation with the trade union or individual workers was entered into, nor were the selection criteria for the redundancies made known. A number of employees, including Mr Williams, selected for compulsory redundancy, complained of unfair dismissal.

Held: (EAT) In making a finding of unfair dismissal, the EAT laid down several aspects of good practice which an employer seeking to make redundancies should follow:

(a) The employer should give as much warning as possible.

(b) The employer should consult with the trade union, particularly regarding selection procedure.

(c) The selection procedure should be objective.

(d) The employer should ensure that the selection procedure is followed.

(e) The employer should seek to offer alternative employment. [1982] I.C.R. 156.

Commentary
The more transparent the selection procedure is, *e.g.* LIFO—last in, first out the more likely it is that the tribunal will not question it (*British Aerospace v Green* [1995] I.C.R. 1006).

Key Principle: **Section 188 of the TULR(C)A imposes a duty on an employer to consult if planning to make more than 20 redundancies within 90 days at any one establishment.**

GMB Union v Man Truck & Bus UK Ltd 2000
In order to harmonise the employment terms and conditions of two groups of workers following a merger, the employer wrote to the workers terminating their existing contracts and offering new terms and conditions. The GMB Union complained to a tribunal that the letter amounted to a dismissal by reason of redundancy and an offer of new employment. As such, under s.188 of the TULR(C)A the company should have consulted before issuing redundancy letters. The employer argued that it

was not their proposal or intention that jobs be lost, and consequently the letters did not amount to dismissals on the grounds of redundancy. At first instance the tribunal agreed with the employer's argument.

Held: (EAT) Although the motivation for the letters may have been the introduction of new terms and conditions, the method by which the new terms were to be introduced involved the termination of existing contracts, which following s.95 of the ERA 1996 amounts to a dismissal, and since those dismissals are not for reasons related to the individual (s.195 of the TULR(C)A), they must be presumed to be for redundancy. [2000] I.R.L.R. 636.

Commentary

There are two important issues here, both covered by statute. Firstly, s.95 of the ERA 1996 has been interpreted to indicate that the motive or reason behind the termination of the contract need not be considered in deciding whether a dismissal has taken place. The words of the statute may be taken literally. Secondly, there is a reminder of the rebuttable presumption that a dismissal is for reason of redundancy unless the contrary is proved (s.195(2) of the TULR(C)A).

Scotch Premier Meat Co Ltd v Burns 2000

The company were faced with major financial problems and had decided that there were only two viable options open to it; either they could sell the company as a going concern, or they could close the company and sell the site to a developer. Closure of the company would result in over 150 redundancies. The company offered all the employees voluntary redundancy in April 1998, which some of the employees accepted. Those employees remaining were made compulsorily redundant in June 1998. No prior consultations were undertaken with the workforce. The issue before the court was whether the company had, at the time of contemplating the two options, "proposed" to make more than 100 workers redundant—if so, since there had been no prior consultation, the company had acted contrary to s.188 of the TULR(C)A.

Held: (EAT) Although "contemplation" of redundancy is sufficient to bring the company's actions within the scope of the EC Directive 98/59 on collective redundancies, s.188 of the TULR(C)A requires that redundancies must be "proposed".

However, on the facts of this case, the EAT held that the tribunal had been entitled to find that the company had "proposed" redundancies at the time of the options plan, and consequently consultations with the workforce should have taken place at that time. [2000] I.R.L.R. 639.

Commentary
Two issues arise out of this case. Firstly, for the purpose of s.188, employees taking voluntary redundancy are "dismissed". Secondly, the EAT did not rule on the question of whether s.188 should be construed in line with the EC Collective Redundancies Directive, holding instead that there were differences between "contemplated" and "proposed". It would therefore appear that until a company's options solidify into actual proposals, no consultation is necessary.

Key Principle: **If an offer of suitable alternative employment is unreasonably refused by the employee, the employee will have no entitlement to a redundancy payment.**

Taylor v Kent County Council 1969
Mr Taylor was headmaster of a school that was merged with another school adjacent. It was decided that as only one head teacher was necessary, Mr Taylor's post was no longer required. Rather than being offered or made redundant, Mr Taylor was offered a post as relief teacher at his existing salary, to be sent as and when required to fill-in at schools within the area. He refused to accept this position, and the employer claimed that as he had refused an offer of suitable alternative employment he was not entitled to a redundancy payment.

Held: (QBD) The court held that for an offer of employment to be an offer of "suitable alternative employment" the terms of the employment should be reasonably equivalent to those of the previous employment. It was not sufficient that the salary should be similar if the employment itself was of an entirely different nature. [1969] 2 Q.B. 560.

Commentary
The court made it clear that "suitable" should include consideration of such factors as status, job location and job content.

John Fowler Ltd v Parkin 1975
The company decided to close down its foundry in Sheffield, and made an offer of "suitable alternative employment" to several of its employees, including Mr Parkin, to work at another factory some 13 miles distant. The tribunal awarded redundancy payments to each of the workers, stating that "we feel it cannot be said that (the men) have unreasonably refused the offer."

Held: (QBD) The tribunal had erred in law by not separately considering the two questions: (a) is the offer of employment an offer of suitable alternative employment, and (b) if so, was the refusal a reasonable refusal. [1975] I.R.L.R. 89.

Commentary
It is important to consider the two stages separately. There are occasions when an offer of suitable employment may be refused, without losing entitlement to a redundancy payment.

---

11. TRANSFER OF UNDERTAKINGS

Key Principle: **The definition of an "undertaking" contained in the Transfer of Undertakings (Protection of Employment) Regulations 1981 as being only a commercial undertaking has been extended by case law to include non-commercial undertakings.**

Dr Sophie Redmond Stichting v Bartol 1992
A Dutch local authority provided grants to run a centre providing counseling and help to drug addicts. The centre was then taken over by another body, the Sigma Foundation. Sigma wished to dismiss some of the original employees, which it could only lawfully do if the centre was not covered by the Acquired Rights Directive (EC/77/187). As the Directive appeared only to apply to commercial organisations, the case was referred to the ECJ.

Held: (ECJ) "(The Directive) ... has the object of guaranteeing the rights of employees, and it applies to all employees who are covered by protection against dismissal..." [1992] I.R.L.R. 366.

Commentary
The ECJ, perhaps not surprisingly, took a purposive approach and held that the Directive should apply in this case to charitable institutions.

Key Principle: **There must be a transfer of the "business", mere transfer of assets may not be sufficient.**

Melon v Hector Powe Ltd 1981
Hector Powe manufactured men's clothing for sale through their own outlets. They owned several factories, one of which they sold to Executex Ltd, a company manufacturing garments on behalf of a number of different customers. The sale included the factory, plant and equipment, plus work in hand at the time of the sale. Although the staff were taken on by Executex, a number of them claimed a redundancy payment from Hector Powe, on the basis that the sale did not amount to a transfer under what is now TUPE 1982.

Held: (HL) Although there were a number of factors which pointed towards a transfer of the business, two factors particularly cast doubt on this. Firstly, Hector Powe manufactured only certain types of clothing, all for sale through their own retail outlets; Executex, on the other hand, manufactured whatever garments its customers required. Secondly, there was no general transfer of assets and liabilities, nor was there a transfer of goodwill. Consequently, the House of Lords decided that the sale did not amount to a transfer, and therefore the staff were entitled to a redundancy payment from Hector Powe. [1981] I.C.R. 43.

Commentary
It may therefore be said that for a sale to qualify as a transfer under TUPE, it should consist of the sale of a business as a going concern, not merely a collection of assets. (See also *Spijkers v Gebroeders Benedik Abattoir CV* [1986] 2 C.M.L.R. 296.)

Dines v Initial Health Care Services 1994
A number of cleaners were employed by Initial to provide services at a particular hospital. When the contract expired it was not renewed with Initial, but awarded to a different

contractor. This new contractor employed the cleaners previously employed by Initial, but at a lower rate of pay. The cleaners argued that their terms and conditions were protected by TUPE Regulations.

Held: (CA) The court held that a relevant transfer had taken place. They argued that the hospital cleaning services were to be carried out by mainly the same operatives, at the same premises and for the same client, therefore for the purposes of the Regulations a transfer of undertakings had occurred. [1994] I.R.L.R. 336.

Commentary
A transfer of undertakings may therefore occur in the event of a compulsory competitive tender (CCT).

Suzen v Zehnacker Gebaudereinigung Krankenhausservice GmbH 1997

The applicant and a number of others were employed as cleaners at a school where Zehnacker had the cleaning contract. Zehnacker then lost the contract to another company and consequently dismissed the cleaners. The cleaners argued that a transfer of undertakings had occurred and their dismissal was unfair.

Held: (ECJ) The court stated that the mere fact that the service provided by the old and new service providers is similar does not support the conclusion that an economic entity has been transferred. It went on to state that the losing of a contract to a competitor cannot by itself indicate the existence of a transfer, since it does not in most cases mean that the losing company has ceased to exist. [1997] I.R.L.R. 255.

Commentary
This decision, that on the facts no transfer had taken place, and the reasoning behind it is very difficult to reconcile with earlier ECJ findings. To try to differentiate between a genuine transfer of a business or part of a business, and the loss of a service contract to a competitor, would not appear to be taking a purposive approach to the Directive. For many service industries, the business amounts to little more than the service contracts it holds and the staff it employs; to lose one or more of those contracts is, in effect, to lose a part of the business. Certainly *Suzen* suggests that transfers may be more difficult to prove the more labour intensive

a business becomes, since *Suzen* appears to impliedly place greater emphasis on the transfer of transfer of physical assets to prove that a relevant transfer has taken place.

Betts v Brintel Helicopters Ltd and KLM Era Helicopters (UK) Ltd 1997

Brintel had provided helicopter services under three contracts to Shell (UK) Ltd. When the contracts expired, Brintel were re-awarded two of them, but the third was won by KLM. KLM did not take over any of Brintel's helicopters or staff, nor did they use the same flying base. Although some of Brintel's staff were re-deployed within Brintel's other operations, some, including Betts, were not. Betts claimed unfair dismissal. The question for the court was whether there had been a transfer of undertakings between Brintel and KLM; if so, the dismissal may well have been unfair under TUPE.

Held: (CA) The court followed the recently decided case of *Suzen*, and held that there had been no transfer. It argued that although the operation of the third contract by Brintel had amounted to an undertaking or economic entity, that undertaking had not been transferred. They reasoned that since very few of Brintel's assets had passed to KLM, there was insufficient evidence to show that the undertaking had retained its identity in the hands of KLM. [1997] I.R.L.R. 361.

Commentary

In this case there is evidence that had Betts and others not claimed for unfair dismissal they may well have been engaged by KLM; arguably this should have strengthened the case that a transfer had taken place. However, the court needed to give full consideration to the recently given judgment of the ECJ in the case of *Suzen*.

ECM (Vehicle Delivery Service) Ltd v Cox 1999

Cox was employed by a company who had a contract to deliver cars imported into the UK. The company lost the contract to ECM who did not employ any of the existing staff, and who operated the contract in a different way and from a different base. Cox and others brought complaints of unfair dismissal, claiming that TUPE applied. Their complaint was upheld by the tribunal, prior to the *Suzen* decision. An appeal to the EAT, following *Suzen*, was dismissed on the grounds that when an employee's employment is contingent upon the existence of a particular contract, the loss of that contract to a competitor may then amount to a transfer of undertakings. The employer then appealed to the Court of Appeal arguing that there can be no transfer if the only continuing feature is the actual service provided—following *Suzen,* a relevant transfer must include at least some of the assets of the transferor.

Held: (CA)

> "Although the *Suzen* decision has been described as involving a shift of emphasis or a clarification of the law, nothing was said in *Suzen* which casts doubt on the correctness of the interpretation of the Directive in the earlier decisions..."

per Mummery L.J. Therefore, the court held, on the facts available to the tribunal it was open to them to conclude that in this case a transfer had taken place. [1999] I.R.L.R. 559.

Commentary
It appears that this is an attempt by a national court to either restrict or purposively interpret the decision in the ECJ case of *Suzen.* It remains to be seen how successful this attempt will be, but it may be argued that the ECJ has already resiled from a strict or restrictive interpretation of *Suzen* in such later cases as *Sanchez Hidalgo* [1999] I.R.L.R. 136.

Key Principle: **Once a relevant transfer has been established, it may be difficult for either the transferor or the transferee to escape liability under TUPE.**

Berriman v Delabole Slate Ltd 1985
Mr Berriman's employers sold their business as a going concern to Delabole Slate, who wished to bring the terms of the transferred employees into line with those of their existing staff. This would result in a decrease in guaranteed pay for Mr Berriman, who rejected the offer, left and complained of unfair dismissal. Initially the tribunal held that the dismissal was for an "economic, technical or organisational reason", and did not therefore constitute unfair dismissal.

Held: (CA) The Court of Appeal took a different view. They held that the reason for the dismissal was that the new employer wished to change employment terms and conditions of the transferred staff, and that "the reason itself does not involve any change either in the number or the functions of the workforce". [1985] I.R.L.R. 305.

Commentary

The court appears to have adopted a purposive approach, and at first glance this decision appears to afford considerable protection to transferred workers. However, the question that needs to be asked is for how long could this situation continue—at what point would a change in the transferred employee's terms cease to be as a result of the transfer, and become a potentially fair SOSR?

Litster v Forth Dry Dock and Engg Co Ltd 1989

The respondent company was in receivership and agreed to dismiss the workforce before the transfer took place so as to make the transfer more attractive to the transferee by attempting to avoid for the transferee any liability under TUPE (the transferor being in receivership and, with the debtors having realised their security, there were insufficient assets to meet the transferor's liability for unfair dismissal or redundancy claims).

Held: (HL) The House of Lords adopted a purposive approach to the legislation however, and stated that Reg.5(3) of TUPE should be read as if the words: "or would have been so employed if he had not been unfairly dismissed..." had been inserted after: "... a person so employed immediately before the transfer..." Thus the dismissed employees were brought within the scope of the Regulations, and the transferee became responsible for their dismissal. [1989] I.C.R. 341.

Commentary

It is, of course, necessary that the unfair dismissal of the employee prior to the transfer can be shown to have been actually brought about by the impending transfer and not for some other reason.

12. RESTRAINT OF TRADE

Key Principle: **If the employee competes with his employer during the existence of a contract of employment, that competition will normally amount to a breach of the duty of fidelity.**

Hivac Ltd v Park Royal Scientific Instruments Ltd 1946

Two of Hivac's employees worked part-time for Park Royal Scientific, a competitor. There was no evidence that the employees had passed on any confidential information to Park Royal, or indeed that they were in any position to do so. Hivac, however, applied for an injunction restraining Park Royal from employing them.

Held: (CA) In granting the injunction, the court sought to balance the opposing views; on the one hand, the right of a workman to spend his leisure time for profit if he wished, and on the other, the right of the employer to protect itself from its employees deliberately harming its business. [1946] Ch 169.

Commentary

This case demonstrates the overlap between the duty of fidelity and the issues of restraint of trade. Generally, the duty of fidelity will be taken to concern competition whilst the contract of employment exists, and restraint of trade concerns the period after the contract has been terminated.

Key Principle: **"Garden leave" is the situation whereby an employee who on termination of his contract of employment with company A may be restrained from working for another employer until the expiry of his notice period, even if company A do not require or allow the employee to attend for work, as long as they continue to pay his salary for the notice period.**

Evening Standard Co Ltd v Henderson 1987

Mr Henderson's contract provided for one year's notice to be given by either party. He terminated his contract, giving only two month's notice, with the intention of working for a rival newspaper. The Evening Standard applied for an injunction restraining him from working for the rival newspaper until the full contractual one year notice period had expired. During the notice period they were quite happy to continue to pay his salary and they did not insist that he should attend for work.

Held: (CA) The court held that the balance of convenience was in favour of granting the injunction and restraining Henderson from taking up his new position whilst the notice period was still current. [1987] I.C.R. 588.

Commentary
It should, however, be remembered that an order of specific performance obliging an employee to work for a particular employer may not be granted (s.236 of the TULR(C)A 1992).

Provident Financial Group plc v Hayward 1989
At the time of his resignation Mr Hayward worked for a firm of estate agents as financial director. Although his contract made provision for 12 months' notice of termination, it was mutually agreed that he need only give six months' notice. He continued to work his notice period for three months, but his employer then decided that he need no longer attend the office although they were prepared to continue to pay him until the notice period expired. The following month he announced his intention to start work with another firm of estate agents. His employers sought an injunction to restrain him from doing so until the expiry of his notice period.

Held: (CA) In this case, the Court of Appeal decided that since there was only some two and a half months of the notice period remaining, and since it was unlikely that any serious damage would result to Provident from Mr Hayward taking up his new appointment immediately, the injunction should be refused. [1989] I.C.R. 160.

Commentary
It is difficult on the bare facts to reconcile this case with the case of *Henderson*, see also the cases of *GFI Group Inc v Eaglestone* [1994] I.R.L.R. 119, and *William Hill Org Ltd v Tucker* [1998] I.R.L.R. 313. The later cases may suggest a reluctance on the part of the courts to enforce "garden leave" clauses.

William Hill Organisation Ltd v Tucker 1999
Mr Tucker worked for William Hill under a contract of employment which specified a six month notice period. Tucker gave

one months' notice of termination with the apparent intention of working for a competitor. William Hill sought to enforce the original notice period by requiring Tucker to take six months' garden leave, during which time his salary would continue to be paid, but he would not be required to work.

Held: (CA) The enforcement of a garden leave clause must be based on similar grounds as the enforcement of a restraint of trade clause. Furthermore, a garden leave clause should not be implied in situations where the employee has an interest in performing the work more than merely earning the money. In the instant case, the imposition of a "garden leave" clause amounted to a breach of contract. [1999] I.C.R. 291.

Commentary
The court is therefore less likely to enforce an *implied* garden leave clause than an *express* one. Moreover, grounds for enforcing a garden leave clause should be no less strict than those for enforcing a restraint of trade clause.

Key Principle: **Restrictive covenants will only be enforced by the courts in so far as they are both necessary to protect an employer's proprietary interests and reasonable in terms of scope, length of time and geographical area.**

Herbert Morris Ltd v Saxelby 1916
Saxelby was an engineer whose contract of employment contained a clause whereby he would not work for any competing company for a period of seven years after the termination of his contract.

Held: (HL) The clause could not be enforced. It amounted to a restriction on the skill and ability he had gained, rather than a safeguard of the company's interest. [1916] A.C. 688.

Commentary
The courts must balance the right of an individual to use their skills against the right of the employer to protect its secrets.

Forster & Sons Ltd v Suggett 1918
Forster was the production manager of a company involved in the competitive industry of glass making. As production

manager, he was privy to many of the company's trade secrets, and his contract of employment contained a clause restricting him from working for a competitor for a five-year period after termination of his contract.

Held: (Q.B.) Because of the secret nature of the manufacturing processes involved, and Forster's level within the company, the clause was enforceable. (1918) 35 T.L.R. 87.

Commentary
The courts therefore consider both the nature of the information held by the employee and the level of his position within the company.

Fitch v Dewes 1921
The employee was a solicitor's clerk whose contract of employment contained a clause restraining him from working in a solicitors office within a seven mile radius of the town centre for the rest of his life.

Held: (HL) The House of Lords held that because of the confidential nature of the business and the relatively restricted geographical area involved, the clause was valid. [1921] 2 A.C. 158.

Commentary
It may be doubted if a lifetime restriction on a solicitor's clerk working in a particular town would be enforceable today.

Rock Refrigeration Ltd v Jones 1997
Jones was employed by Rock under a contract of employment which contained a clause restricting Jones' future employment for a period of one year following termination of his contract "howsoever occasioned". Jones left Rock and went to work for a competitor. Rock sought to enforce the clause, but the court held that the clause amounted to an unreasonable restraint of trade and should fail.

Held: (CA) It was not necessarily the case that a clause restricting an employee's future employment was unreasonable and thus unenforceable. If the contract had been terminated by the employer committing a repudiatory breach, then, following *General Billposting Co v Atkinson* [1909] A.C. 118, the clause may

not be enforceable. However, the clause would remain binding
if either the breach did not amount to a repudiatory breach, or if
the breach was not accepted by the employee. [1997] I.C.R. 938.

Commentary
This case overruled the earlier case of *D v M* [1996] I.R.L.R. 192,
which purported to hold that a restrictive covenant amounted to
an unreasonable restraint of trade, and as such may be
unenforceable.

Faccenda Chicken v Fowler 1986
Mr Fowler had worked for Faccenda as sales manager before he
left and set up his own business in competition, employing
several other Faccenda ex-employees. Between them they had
information as to the names and addresses of Faccenda's
customers, amounts of their orders and the prices charged.
Faccenda argued that this was confidential information, and
Fowler should be restrained from using it.

Held: (CA)

> "It is clear that the obligation not to use or disclose
> information may cover secret processes ... and other infor-
> mation which is of a sufficiently high degree of con-
> fidentiality as to amount to a trade secret. The obligation
> does not extend, however, to cover all information which is
> given to or acquired by the employee while in his employ-
> ment, and in particular may not cover information which is
> only "confidential"..." [1986] I.C.R. 297.

Commentary
The judgment is worth reading in full for the distinctions it draws
between "trade secrets" and other information, which whilst being
"confidential", may not be protected once the employment is
terminated.

13. TRADE UNIONS

Definition of a "trade union"

Key Principle: A broad definition of a trade union is included in s.1 of the Trade Union and Labour Relations (Consolidation) Act 1992, but this definition is strictly applied.

Midland Cold Storage Ltd v Turner 1972 : Midland Cold Storage Ltd v Steer 1972
Both of these cases were heard on the same set of facts; the case of *Turner* is the one most often quoted. The case concerned the status of a shop stewards' committee—did the committee constitute a trade union, if so, several of its acts would then be protected by legislation. It appeared that the main function of the committee was the recommending and organising of industrial action in the London docks. There was no evidence that the committee was involved in negotiations with the employers—which was left to the established trade union organisation—or that they had sought recognition from the employers.

Held: (NIRC) The court agreed that the committee was an "organisation" and that it consisted wholly or mainly of workers—both requirements under the legislation. However, the fact that the committee had not sought recognition from the employer indicated to the court that the principle object of the committee could not include the regulation of relations between workers and employers. Consequently, the committee could not be held to fulfill the necessary definition of a trade union. [1972] I.C.R. 773.

Commentary
As such the committees actions were not protected by legislation. The court adopted a straight-forward, but strict approach to the interpretation of, what is now, s.1 of the TULR(C)A.

Legal status of trade unions

Key Principle: The status of a trade union is defined in s.10 of the TULR(C)A as a quasi-corporate body.

EETPU v Times Newspapers 1980

The trade union brought an action for defamation against the owners of the Times Newspaper in respect of statements printed in the paper. The question for the court was whether a trade union could maintain an action for damages for defamation in its own name.

Held: (QBD) As a libel is a wrong against a person, and not a wrong against property, only if a trade union has a separate legal personality may it sue for libel on itself. Section 10 of TULC(R)A makes it clear that a trade union may not be treated as if it were a body corporate. Therefore a trade union does not have status to maintain an action for defamation to its own reputation. [1980] 1 All E.R. 1097.

Commentary

In this case, O'Connor J. stated that he believed that everyone—except the law—would say that a trade union has a separate reputation which it should be allowed to protect. However, the words of the statute are clear on this issue.

Trade union independence

Key Principle: **An "independent trade union" is one which is not under the control or domination of an employer, nor liable to interference from an employer.**

Blue Circle Staff Association v Certification Officer 1977

The particular facts of this case are unimportant. The importance of the case concerns the guidance given by the court, in the form of criteria, to Certification Officers when assessing the independence of a trade union.

Held: (EAT) The following criteria and comments were given:

(a) Finance: If there is any evidence that the union is getting direct finance from the employer, the union is not independent.

(b) Other assistance: The CO should examine whether the union receives other assistance from the company, possibly by way of free office space, time off for officials, etc.

(c) Employer interference: If the union is small and weak and gets help from the employer, its independence must be in doubt.

(d) History: The history of a union is important; sometimes unions may grow from management-run staff associations.

(e) Rules: The union rule book is scrutinised. Can the employer interfere with, or even control the union?

(f) Single company unions: Although not debarred from obtaining independent status, a single company union is more susceptible to employer interference.

(g) Organisation: The CO should examine the union structure, its recruiting ability, its finances and its officers.

(h) Attitude: The CO looks for a "robust attitude in negotiation" as a sign of genuine independence. [1977] 1 W.L.R. 239.

Commentary
The above criteria are an indication of the way in which a Certification Officer may go about deciding whether a trade union is genuinely independent from the employer.

Squibb UK Staff Association v Certification Officer 1979
Staff from Squibb & Sons had formed a staff association consisting of some 230 out of a possible 290 workers. The employer had provided free office accommodation and free administrative facilities. When they applied for independent status three years later, the Certification Officer refused their application on the grounds that the union was "liable to interference" from the employer.

Held: (CA) The question for the court was whether the words "liable to interference" may mean merely "vulnerable to interference", or whether they must mean "likely to interference". If the former, then the union may still gain independent status following the criteria of *Blue Circle*, if the latter, the Certification Officer had grounds for refusing. The court, Lord Denning M.R., argued that it was sufficient that the employer could interfere to the point of control; it was not necessary to show that the employer intended influencing the union. Consequently, the application for independent status should be rejected. [1979] 1 W.L.R. 523.

Commentary
This clearly demonstrates the difficulty faced by small single
company unions in their attempt to gain independent status.

Union recognition

Key Principle: **Prior to the introduction of the Employment
Relations Act 1999, recognition of a union by the employer
was a question almost exclusively for the employer.**

NUGSAT v Albury Bros Ltd 1978
A small number of the company's employees became members
of NUGSAT union. Shortly afterwards, the union district official
had discussions with the company concerning the rates of pay
of one of the employees. When the company made a number of
employees redundant without any prior consultation, the union
argued that it had a statutory right to be consulted prior to any
redundancies, under what is now TULR(C)A 1992. The company argued that the union had no such right, since the union
was not officially recognised by the company.

Held: (CA) The court held that merely being involved in one
meeting did not amount to recognition. Recognition must be
either agreed by the parties, or must consist of a sufficiently
clear course of conduct that an observer would appreciate that
the union and the company had recognised one another for the
purpose of collective bargaining. [1978] I.R.L.R. 504.

Commentary
This approach was also taken in the case of *USDAW v Sketchley
Ltd* [1981] I.R.L.R. 291. It must be noted that there are provisions
within the ERA 1999 for automatic recognition of a trade union
by an employer, normally if either a majority of the workers in the
bargaining unit are members of the trade union, or 40 per cent of
those workers in the bargaining unit are voting in favour of
recognition. The procedure for recognition and any balloting
necessary is supervised by the Central Arbitration Committee
(CAC).

Time off for union activities

Key Principle: **An employer must allow an employee who is a member of an independent recognised trade union time off to take part in union activities.**

Luce v Bexley LBC 1990

During the passage through Parliament of the 1988 Education Reform Bill, the National Union of Teachers requested that a number of teachers employed by Bexley should be allowed time off to lobby Parliament. When the employer refused, an action was brought claiming that the employer's refusal amounted to a breach of s.170 of the TULR(C)A.

Held: (EAT) Although statute makes provision for time off for trade union activities, not all activities of a political or ideological nature will be covered. The term "trade union activity" covers a very broad range of activity, and the court did not exclude the possibility that some activity directed towards Parliament should be covered. Nevertheless, on the information available to them, the tribunal had been entitled to find that in this case there was no breach of the provisions of TULR(C)A by the employer. [1990] I.R.L.R. 422.

Commentary

This case is slightly unusual in that the applicant refused either to give evidence personally, or to call any witnesses. It appears from the law report that had further information been available to the tribunal, a different decision may well have been reached.

Trade union political fund

Key Principle: **If the trade union wishes to contribute towards political ends, such contribution must come from a separate political fund.**

Birch v National Union of Railwaymen 1950

The NUR rulebook contained a rule that only those members contributing to the political fund may take part in the management of that fund. Mr Birch was elected as a local branch official, part of whose duties was an involvement in the management of the political fund. As Mr Birch chose not to contribute to this fund, the management of the union argued that he was not eligible for office, since he would be unable to fulfil all the requisite duties.

Held: (ChD) The court held that the rule concerning the political fund offended against, what is now, s.82(1) of the TULR(C)A. Whereas it was reasonable that only those members who contributed to the political fund should have authority to manage the fund, it was quite another thing that the rule should have the effect of disqualifying anyone not contributing to the fund from holding office of almost any sort within the union. [1950] Ch 602.

Commentary
One effect of this judgment is that unions must keep the political fund totally separate from other union funds.

Paul v NALGO 1987
NALGO had organised a publicity campaign during the run-up to a general election, focusing on the policies of the government. As the union, at that time, did not have a political fund, an action was brought by a number of its members complaining that the campaign was unlawful, being expenditure for political objectives—which according to, what is now, s.72 of the TULR(C)A could only be made from a political fund.

Held: (ChD) Despite the fact that the posters and leaflets contained a disclaimer saying that the reader was not being urged to vote in a particular way, the court held that the real purpose of the campaign was to influence people into voting against the policies of the Conservative Party. As such, it amounted to political expenditure which could only be made from the political fund. [1987] I.R.L.R. 413.

Commentary
It may therefore be difficult for any union which does not run a separate political fund to organise a campaign against government policies. To do so successfully, it would have to show that the motivation and objectives of the campaign are not political.

Freedom of association

Young, James and Webster v United Kingdom 1981

At the time, British Rail—along with many other employers within the UK—operated a closed shop. Employment within British Rail was only permitted if the employee joined the appropriate trade union, should he refuse to join or subsequently leave the union, his employment would terminate. The three plaintiffs had all refused to join the trade union and had been dismissed by British Rail. They took their case to the European Court of Human Rights.

Held: (ECtHR) The court held that the right to form or join a trade union is the fundamental aspect of freedom of association. Conversely, therefore, the right not to join or to leave a union must also form part of the basic right of freedom of association. The actions of British Rail supported by the domestic legislation of the UK therefore breached Art.11 of the Convention. [1981] I.R.L.R. 408.

Commentary

Two issues should be remembered; firstly, following TULR(C)A 1992, the closed shop principle is no longer legally enforceable in the UK. Secondly, this case took place before judgments of the ECHR had effect in UK courts or legislation.

Wilson v United Kingdom; Palmer v United Kingdom 2002

Both Mr Wilson and Mr Palmer had been offered, but refused, a pay rise by their respective employer if they would sign individual contracts of employment and terminate their existing contracts which included collective bargaining agreements with their trade unions. They both brought claims, arguing *inter alia* that the employers purpose had been to deter them from belonging to a trade union contrary to (then) s.23(1)(a) of the Employment Protection (Consolidation) Act 1978. The cases went as far as the House of Lords ([1995] I.R.L.R. 258) which found against Wilson and Palmer, holding that collective bargaining was not a defining characteristic of trade union membership. They complained to the ECtHR that the actions of the UK courts had breached their rights under Art.11 of the ECHR.

Held: (ECtHR) The court held that although the absence of a requirement in UK law for companies to enter into collective bargaining did not give rise to a breach of Art.11 of the

Convention, the offering by employers of incentives to employees for the relinquishing of important trade union rights did amount to a breach of Art.11. (2002) 35 E.H.R.R. 20.

Commentary
The judgment reinforces the right to freedom of association. Although stopping short of suggesting that employees may have a positive right to take industrial action, the court made clear that employees must be free to instruct or permit their trade union to take such steps as were necessary to promote their interests.

Union rules

Key Principle: **Union rules and disciplinary procedures are open to scrutiny by the courts.**

Lee v The Showmen's Guild of Great Britain 1952
A dispute took place between Lee and another showman concerning a particular "pitch" or site at a fairground. A local union committee resolved the dispute in favour of the other party, Lee refused to accept this decision, took the site himself, and was fined £100 by the union committee. He refused to pay and sought assistance from the court in preventing the Guild from expelling him.

Held: (CA) The court held that the jurisdiction of a domestic tribunal, such as a union committee, must be founded on a contract, and the extent of the jurisdiction must be contained within a set of rules. Furthermore, the contract must be constrained both by issues of public policy and natural justice. It therefore follows that breach of any of these issues would entitle the courts to intervene. In the instant case, Lee had been threatened with expulsion for breach of a rule concerning unfair competition. The court found that, although Lee had acted badly and should have accepted the original decision of the union committee, on the facts there was no issue of unfair competition and consequently the union had no jurisdiction to find him guilty of it. [1952] 2 Q.B. 329.

Commentary
Commentators have noted that the power of the courts to interfere with the internal running of a trade union seems to be

rather greater than the powers of an employment tribunal to question the actions of an employer.

Roebuck v National Union of Mineworkers (Yorkshire Area) (No.2) 1978

Arthur Scargill, later president of the NUM, had, on behalf of the union, successfully brought an action against a newspaper. At the court hearing two members of the NUM had spoken on behalf of the newspaper. After the trial Mr Scargill prepared a report which was most strongly critical of the actions of the two men. The union area executive laid charges against the two men, which were found proved, and this was confirmed by the union area council. Although he had not voted on the outcome of the disciplinary proceedings, Mr Scargill was president of both committees and had spoken in the deliberations. The two men applied to the courts for an injunction to prevent punishment taking place against them.

Held: (ChD) Because of his particular involvement in the matter, Mr Scargill should not have acted as chairman in the disciplinary proceedings. There was an inevitable appearance of bias, and the likelihood of bias was probable. [1978] I.C.R. 676.

Commentary
The rules of natural justice must therefore apply to any union disciplinary measures.

14. INDUSTRIAL CONFLICT

Key Principle: **"Industrial action" covers not only strike action, but also refusal to undertake non-contractual overtime working.**

Faust v Power Packing Casemakers Ltd 1983

Employees dismissed for refusing to work non-contractual overtime brought a claim for unfair dismissal, which was upheld by the tribunal.

Held: (CA) A refusal to work non-contractual overtime could amount to "industrial action". That being the case, particularly

142   Employment Law

if such action were unofficial action, the tribunal would have no
jurisdiction to hear the case. [1983] I.R.L.R. 117.

Commentary
In such a situation, the motive of the employee is important. If the
reason for the action were to put pressure on the employer, the
court would be justified in holding that it amounted to industrial
action; whereas, if the motive were to attend a function, or take
part in an event of some sort, the court would have difficulty in
labeling the refusal as industrial action.

Key Principle: **There are four major economic torts for which,
in certain situations, the union may escape all liability.**

Inducement of breach of contract

Lumley v Gye 1853
An opera singer had a contract to perform exclusively at a
particular theatre for a period of three months. She was persuaded by the defendant to break the contract and appear at
another theatre. Although, at the time, there was a tort of the
"enticement of a servant", it was doubtful if the singer could be
said to be the servant of the plaintiff theatre manager.

Held: (QBD) The tort was extended to situations where "the
wrongful interruption operates to prevent the service during the
time for which the parties have contracted that the service shall
continue". (1853) 2 E&B 216.

Commentary
In terms of industrial action, the tort may cover not only breach of
an employment contract, but also breach of a company's contract
with a third party.

DC Thomson & Co Ltd v Deakin 1952
The company refused to employ union labour, and dismissed a
worker who joined a printing union. The union called on
workers in other companies and industries to support them,
with the effect that drivers for the company Bowaters, who
supplied Thomsons with paper, refused to handle deliveries for
Thomsons. To avoid industrial problems of their own, Bowaters

did not instruct their drivers to make deliveries to Thomsons. Thomsons sought an injunction preventing the trade union from seeking to cause a breach of the contract between Bowaters and Thomsons.

Held: (CA) The court held that the tort would be committed if four elements were proven: (1) if the person charged with committing the tort knew of the existence of the contract and intended its breach, (2) that the person so charged did induce the breach of the contract, (3) that the employees so persuaded did breach their contracts of employment, and (4) that the breaches of the employees' contracts did cause breach of the contract complained of. In the instant case the tort had not been committed since, as Bowaters had not directly instructed their drivers to deliver to Thomsons, the drivers had not breached their contracts of employment. [1952] Ch 646.

Commentary
A direct inducement to breach of contract, as in *Lumley v Gye* will always constitute a tort, but an indirect inducement will only amount to a tort if unlawful means are used.

Interference with contract or trade

Torquay Hotel Co Ltd v Cousins 1969
Esso had a contract for the supply of heating oil to the hotel. A clause in the contract stated that Esso would not be liable if they were prevented from fulfilling the contract due to labour disputes. Esso were advised that the Imperial Hotel was "blacked" following a labour dispute involving the Transport and General Workers Union and various hotels in the area. As a result Esso did not supply oil to the hotel. An argument that the actions of the trade union had led to the indirect form of the tort of inducement to breach of contract must surely fail, since, due to the inclusion of the clause, there had been no breach of contract.

Held: (CA) Finding that a tort had been committed, the Court of Appeal held that either, there may be liability for interfering with the contract short of breach—*per* Lord Denning M.R.; or that the exclusion clause related to liability for non-performance, rather than to obligation to perform—*per* Russell L.J.; or there would be liability if the normal course of dealing had led the parties to expect performance—*per* Winn L.J. [1969] 2 Ch 106.

Commentary
This decision amounts to a considerable extension to the tort of inducement to breach of contract as laid down in *Thomson v Deakin*.

Merkur Island Shipping Corp. v Laughton 1983
The plaintiffs were owners of a Liberian registered ship crewed by a mainly Filipino crew, who were apparently paid less than the internationally agreed wages. When the ship was ready to sail from Liverpool docks, the union persuaded the tugmen to refuse to move her out of the dock. The ship owners sought an injunction based upon interference with the performance of the contract requiring the union to lift its "blacking" of the ship. (It may have been possible to cite the tort of inducement to breach of contract since the tugmen were in breach of their contract of employment, but as in *Torquay Hotel*, the charter contained an exclusion clause.)

Held: (HL) The House of Lords approved the reasoning of Lord Denning in the *Torquay Hotels* case, and confirmed the existence of, in effect, a separate tort of interference with contract or trade as an extension of the indirect form of the tort of inducement to breach of contract. [1983] 2 A.C. 570.

Commentary
This is obviously a wide reaching judgment in that it has been suggested that it creates a "super-tort". It is very possible that the full effects of this tort are still to be seen.

Intimidation

Rookes v Barnard 1964
BOAC, one of the predecessors of British Airways, operated at that time a closed shop agreement with a trade union, the AESD. One of the employees, Mr Rookes, resigned from the union. The union threatened BOAC with industrial action if they continued to employ a non-union worker. BOAC therefore issued Rookes with notice of termination of his contract of employment. Rookes then brought an action against the union officials for intimidation.

Held: (HL)

> "The question in this case is whether it was unlawful for them (the union) to use a threat to break their contracts with

the employer as a weapon to make him (BOAC) do something which he was legally entitled to do but which they knew would cause loss to (Rookes)."—*per* Lord Reid.

"I find therefore nothing to differentiate a threat of a breach of contract from a threat of physical violence or other illegal threat."—*per* Lord Devlin.

Thus, the House of Lords found the existence of a tort of intimidation, and on the facts of the case the union officials had committed the tort. [1964] A.C. 1129.

Commentary
At the time, this decision was a major threat to trade unions, since there was no immunity from the tort of intimidation. Such an immunity now exists within TULR(C)A 1992.

Conspiracy

Quinn v Leatham 1901
Trade union action was threatened against Quinn if he continued to employ non-union labour. The action resulted in the loss of one of Quinn's customers, and Quinn sued for conspiracy to injure.

Held: (HL) All that is required for the tort is that the action by two or more people results in the deliberate injury complained of. [1901] A.C. 495.

Commentary
It should be remembered that at the time the courts did not hold that trade union objectives were legitimate objectives.

Crofter Hand Woven Harris Tweed Co v Veitch 1942
The plaintiffs imported spun yarn from the mainland to the Isle of Lewis for finishing and onward sale as Harris Tweed. Their activities undercut prices of locally spun and woven cloth, and threatened the income of workers, many of whom were members of TGWU. The union called on members who were dockworkers to refuse to handle the plaintiff's goods. The plaintiff then sued the union officials in the tort of conspiracy to injure.

Held: (HL) In dismissing the appeal, the House of Lords held that if the predominant objective of the action taken by the union was to benefit its members by preventing under-cutting and stabilising the economy of the island, no actionable tort would have been committed. [1942] A.C. 435.

Commentary
Thus, if the predominant purpose of the action is not to injure, there will be no actionable tort committed.

Lonrho plc v Fayed 1991
A bid for the House of Fraser chain of stores by Lonrho was referred to the Monopolies Commission, during which time Lonrho agreed not to purchase further shares. At the same time, a rival bid by the Fayed brothers was successful. In an action brought against the Fayed brothers by Lonrho the issue of the tort of conspiracy to injure by unlawful means was brought up.

Held: (HL)

"... when conspirators intentionally injure the plaintiff and use unlawful means to do so, it is no defence for them to show that their primary purpose was to further their own interests; it is sufficient to make their action tortious that the means used were unlawful."—*per* Lord Bridge. [1992] 1 A.C. 448.

Commentary
It should be born in mind that, when considering trade union law, if the unlawful means is protected by immunity, it is not possible to bring a successful action for conspiracy to use them (*Hadmor Productions Ltd v Hamilton* [1982] I.R.L.R. 102).

Key Principle: **Actions by a trade union amounting to one of the four economic torts will be protected if carried out "in contemplation or furtherance of a trade dispute". However, the dispute must relate "wholly or mainly" to one of the matters listed in s.244 of the TULR(C)A.**

Mercury Communications Ltd v Scott-Garner and the POEU 1984
The break-up of the Post Office monopoly on telecommunications in UK allowed for the setting up of British Telecom and

the involvement of private companies, including Mercury Communications. The Post Office Engineering Union was opposed to the policy and instructed its members to refuse to connect Mercury to the existing telephone systems. The union claimed their action had trade dispute immunity, Mercury argued that it was political action.

Held: (CA) The court held that the predominant purpose of the action was opposition to the political policy to liberalise the telecommunications industry—consequently the union action did not enjoy the immunity of a trade dispute. [1983] I.R.L.R. 494.

Commentary
The court accepted that protection of jobs may have been one of the reasons for the dispute, but did not accept that it was a major one.

Key Principle: **Immunity for picketing only extends to those picketing at or near their workplace.**

Rayware Ltd v Transport and General Workers Union 1989
Rayware's factory was on a private industrial estate accessed by a private road over half a mile from the public highway. During an industrial dispute pickets formed at the junction of the public and private road, as close as they could without committing trespass, but some 1,000 yards from their actual place of work. At first instance the court held that the picketing was unlawful, not being "at or near the place of work".

Held: (CA) The court held that the pickets were assembled at the closest point to the plaintiff's factory at which they could lawfully stand, thus they were at or near their place of work. [1989] I.R.L.R. 134.

Commentary
The contrary argument was that the purpose of picketing was to make the employer aware of the dispute and consequently the picketing should take place in very close proximity to the place of work, also since other companies occupied the trading estate they might also be affected by the presence of the pickets. On the facts of the case, the Court of Appeal did not find these arguments sufficiently strong.

Thomas v National Union of Mineworkers 1985

The case concerned the issue of mass picketing and considered whether a group of pickets of between 50–70 miners should be entitled to protection. Arguments had previously been raised (*e.g.* in *Broome v DPP* [1974] I.C.R. 84) that given the presence of an unreasonably large number of pickets, the court would readily infer that their presence was designed not merely to inform but to intimidate.

Held: (ChD) The court held that a picket line of up to six people may have the protection of the law, but large numbers of pickets could not be said to be attending merely to communicate information, their purpose was to intimidate or threaten, and as such they would not enjoy that protection. [1985] I.R.L.R. 136.

Commentary

The court decided on the arbitrary number of six as a potential maximum number of pickets permitted at any one time if protection for their action was not to be lost.

News Group Newspapers Ltd v SOGAT 82 1986

The case arose out of the decision of the Murdoch group of newspapers to move their operation from central London to Wapping. Industrial action resulted in dismissal notices being issued to workers, some of whom then picketed the new works at Wapping. One of the questions raised was whether those pickets dismissed from the central London works enjoyed immunity for picketing "at or near their place of work", since none of them had actually been employed at Wapping.

Held: (QBD) The court held that those picketing at the Wapping plant who did not or had not worked at that plant would be committing the tort of interference with contract and would not be protected by immunity, since Wapping was not at or near their place of work. [1986] I.R.L.R. 337.

Commentary

The judgment is worth reading in full. Along with the case of *Thomas v NUM* it covers most of the issues raised by workers taking industrial action. Arguably, both cases also demonstrate policy or political considerations.

Key Principle: **Certain types of behaviour will give rise to criminal liability for picketing.**

Piddington v Bates 1960

The number of pickets at an industrial dispute had been limited by the police to two at each entrance. Piddington was repeatedly told by the police that two pickets were sufficient and that he was not permitted to join them. He "then pushed gently past (the police officer) and was gently arrested" for obstructing a police officer in the execution of his duty, contrary to what is now s.51 of the Police Act 1964.

Held: (QBD) The police were entitled to hold that two was a sufficient number of pickets, and that more than that number would lead to a real possibility of a breach of the peace. Consequently Piddington had been rightly convicted. [1960] 3 All E.R. 660.

Commentary

Note that it was not suggested that a breach of the peace had occurred, nor that the pickets had offered any threat of violence or were causing any obstruction.

Tynan v Balmer 1967

A group of 40 pickets were organised into a continuously moving circle crossing the public highway outside their employer's factory. When the organiser was requested by the police to stop the moving line he refused and was arrested.

Held: (QBD) The court reiterated that the only lawful activity of a picket was to peacefully obtain or communicate information and to peacefully persuade workers to either work or abstain from working. On the facts of the present case it was found that one of the objects of the pickets was to block the highway and force vehicles approaching the factory to stop. Their activities therefore amounted to an unreasonable use of the highway. [1967] 1 Q.B. 91.

Commentary

It is therefore apparent that the only "rights" of pickets may be strictly limited. See also the case of *Broome v DPP* [1974] I.C.R. 84, where a picket was arrested for standing in front of a lorry attempting to deliver materials to a building site, on the charge of obstructing the highway.

INDEX